LLOYD'S LONDON

AN OUTLINE

BY

M. M. BEEMAN

Constance Smith

1937

(COPYRIGHT)

FIRST EDITION 1937
SECOND EDITION 1938
THIRD EDITION 1938
FOURTH EDITION (REVISED) 1947

PRINTED IN GREAT BRITAIN AT THE WINDMILL PRESS
KINGSWOOD, SURREY

MAIN ENTRANCE TO LLOYD'S

CONTENTS

ILLUSTRATIONS AND PLATES

FOR THE READER'S GUIDANCE

THE AIM of this Outline is to answer some of the questions which are frequently asked by people who wish to know more about Lloyd's and its Members' activities in the fields of Insurance—especially against Non-Marine risks.

Chapter I (Preliminary Remarks) and the first few pages of Chapter II (The Beginnings of Lloyd's) are in the nature of a synopsis of the information given in subsequent Chapters—which may prove to be too detailed for some Readers.

Some of the stock criticisms which at times are levelled against Lloyd's by ill-informed persons are dealt with in Chapter VIII (Opposition to Lloyd's)—whilst Chapter VI (dealing with Lloyd's reputation for fair dealing) also has more than a little bearing on this question.

Probably next in interest from the point of view of the general Reader comes Chapter IX (Miscellaneous).

Apart from the foregoing and Chapter X (dealing with the security behind all Lloyd's Policies), the remaining Chapters are more especially intended for Readers who themselves are actively engaged in Insurance Circles, and whose activities bring them into close contact with Lloyd's.

With a view to emphasising some of the far from commonplace characteristics of Lloyd's it has seemed desirable to seek comparisons between various of its methods and those of the ordinary Insurance Company. However, doing this is rather like trying to compare, say, an automobile with a railway train—on the grounds that each provides a means of transport.

Just as each type of locomotion plays its part and is complementary to others in the fields of Transport, so it may be said that in the World Insurance Market, Lloyd's (as one section) and other great Insurance Organisations (as another section) are each the complement of the other, each in its own way rendering valuable services to the Insuring Public.

The Author would further emphasise that responsibility for any statements made herein lies upon him alone and that any opinions set out in this Outline regarding any of the matters with which it deals must be considered solely as expressing his own personal views—and he sincerely thanks those various friends (amongst whom are certain of his competitors at Lloyd's) who have materially assisted him in its preparation.

Shortly before his death the Author decided to bring the book up to date. The present edition contains his revisions made chiefly with a view to correcting the statistical information. Reference is also made to the new Assurance Companies Act, 1946.

CHAPTER I

Preliminary Remarks

ALTHOUGH the name of "Lloyd's" is widely known in all civilised communities of the present day, it is safe to say that the vast majority of individuals if asked "What is Lloyd's?" could say little more than that it is some kind of organisation that has "something to do with shipping and insurance." A certain number could also be counted upon to describe it, quite incorrectly, as "the Insurance Company with which a person can insure against anything."

That there should be this ignorance regarding what, from the combined aspects of age and size, is one of the most remarkable commercial institutions in the world is, at first sight, rather strange, but in all probability it can be explained by the fact that until towards the end of the last century the activities of Lloyd's were, to all intents, confined to matters connected with Marine Insurance and Shipping. Such subjects are of but little direct interest to most people. They seldom, if ever, give them more than a passing thought, and they neither realise nor really care that for some two centuries before the year 1900 Lloyd's and its activities were—as they still are—an all important and world-wide influence and factor in shipping circles and in the carrying on and development of Marine Insurance.

However, towards the end of the last century the Insurance activities of Lloyd's began to expand into wider fields, and instead of handling only Marine Insurance certain individuals —who at that time were thought by many of their fellow Lloyd's Members to be rash in the extreme—began to transact a very limited volume of other types of Insurance (such as fire, burglary and so on) which can best be described by the comprehensive term of Non-Marine Insurance. For some years the growth of Non-Marine Insurance at Lloyd's was comparatively slow but it had taken firm root by the early years of the present century. Since then its development has proceeded by remarkably rapid stages with the result that for a number of years past Lloyd's has been widely recognised as a very important factor in the world's market for Non-Marine Insurance.

With the advent of Lloyd's into these realms, many Merchants and others who for long had recognised that first-class security was afforded by Lloyd's Marine Policies showed themselves in no way reluctant to take advantage of the further and more novel Insurance facilities which they came to find were obtainable at Lloyd's. They were satisfied that the high standards which prevailed at Lloyd's in regard to Marine Insurance would equally govern its activities in the direction of Non-Marine Insurance. The inner workings of Lloyd's were of little interest to them, they took for granted that the security offered was the same as in the past—and this was sufficient for them.

It is not to these established holders of Lloyd's Policies that this Outline is addressed, although possibly any of them who read it may be interested in learning more about that rather mystifying place or organisation called "Lloyd's" which, in spite of being little more than a name to them has deservedly earned their confidence.

Rather it is addressed to that very large and ever-growing body of people who, although in no way concerned in Marine Insurance matters, are evincing more and more interest in the facilities which Lloyd's nowadays offers in regard to innumerable types of Non-Marine Insurance.

Amongst this very considerable class of people it is natural that there should be many who, before deciding to effect Insurances at Lloyd's, will ask: "What really is Lloyd's?" and "What financial security is there behind a Lloyd's Policy?" It is our purpose to deal with these two questions.

The latter question, dealing as it does with definite facts and figures, can be satisfactorily answered with little difficulty, but to give a brief and at the same time lucid explanation of what Lloyd's really is and how it functions is much more difficult. It must be remembered that Lloyd's, London, is an institution which is unique—in the fullest sense—and without its counterpart anywhere in the world, so that one cannot properly compare it with any well-known type of organisation working along lines which are readily recognised and understood by a large circle of the public.

Equally unique are many of the customs pertaining to the handling of Insurance business at Lloyd's. Some of these customs, if viewed in the light of ordinary everyday business methods by anyone who had not been brought up in the atmosphere of Lloyd's would seem almost inexplicable; and some would certainly seem most unsuitable for employment by any other Insurance Organisation either in this country or abroad—yet the fact remains that it is largely because of these time-tested customs which, with various "unwritten laws," have been slowly developing over more than two centuries that Lloyd's occupies the outstanding position which it now holds.

No description, detailed though it may be, of what may be termed the machinery of Lloyd's can convey any real idea of what Lloyd's actually is and how it works. Thus, whilst in the following Chapters an attempt is made to describe the principal operations which arise in the handling of business at Lloyd's, it must ever be borne in mind that the high repute and respect which it enjoys is largely attributable to that indefinable characteristic which permeates and influences all its operations and which can best be described as the Spirit of Lloyd's.

*   *   *   *   *

Before proceeding to the remaining Chapters in this Outline, it may perhaps be as well that the Reader should realise the following briefly mentioned but salient facts:

1. In the whole world there is only one Lloyd's—that is Lloyd's, London. Lloyd's is *not* an "Insurance Company" but it *is* a unique Insurance Centre which had its beginnings over two centuries ago. (pp. 21, 22.)

2. In various Countries outside Britain sundry insurance organisations exist calling themselves "Lloyds." None of these has any connection with the real Lloyd's and neither in their methods of working nor in their financial structures have any of these self-styled "Lloyds" any resemblance to the real Lloyd's. (p. 75.)

3. Anyone who knows little or nothing about Lloyd's but who wishes to get some understanding of it should commence by thinking of it merely as a place of business or market place (pp. 14, 28–34.)

4. At this place are numerous individuals (Underwriters) who are Members of a Society. The legal name of this Society is the *"Corporation of Lloyd's"* but it is commonly spoken of merely as "Lloyd's." (p. 18.)

5. The Society, i.e. the Corporation of Lloyd's, does not itself undertake any insurance business. When a Lloyd's Policy is issued the insurance which it affords is undertaken by individual Members of Lloyd's who subscribe or underwrite the policy. (pp. 21, 76.)

6. Lloyd's (that is the Society or Corporation of Lloyd's) is specifically recognised by the British Government which has passed special Laws, notably Schedule 8 of the Assurance Companies Act of 1909, designed to ensure that all its *individual* Members shall at all times be able to meet their financial obligations towards holders of any policies which, as Members of Lloyd's, they subscribe under the provisions of that Act. (p. 94.)

7. The application of these Laws is partly in the hands of the Committee of Lloyd's which is recognised by the British Government for this purpose. However, the regulations which the Committee imposes on all Members with a view to safeguarding all holders of Lloyd's Policies go far beyond even the strict requirements of the Law. (p. 95.)

8. Before anyone can be elected as an Underwriting Member of Lloyd's a searching enquiry is made into his standing and financial position and he has to make a substantial Deposit which is held in trust as security solely for his underwriting liabilities. (p. 97.)

9. There are at present about 2300 Members of Lloyd's, the aggregate value of their individual Deposits being substantially in excess of £24,000,000. A Member's Deposit must not be regarded as corresponding to the Share Capital of an Insurance Company—it is more in the nature of a Cash Surplus. (pp. 30, 98.)

10. In addition, all premiums received by a Member have to be paid into a Premium Trust Fund from which they cannot be released (except for the payment of claims and certain underwriting expenses) until all liabilities under the insurances to which they relate have been fully provided for. (p. 99.)

11. Far more important than the existence of these

Deposits and Premium Trust Funds is the fact that the Underwriting Accounts of each Member are subjected at least once annually to a very searching examination by an independent certificated Accountant approved by the Committee. This examination, although colloquially called "the Audit," is infinitely more drastic than the accounting process ordinarily termed an audit. (pp. 93, 103.)

12. "The Audit" is a unique system of proved efficiency designed to ensure that the operations of *any Member who was overtrading or conducting business at a loss would automatically be stopped long before his imprudence could imperil the safety of any Holder of a Lloyd's policy.* (pp. 103–109.)

13. Furthermore, every Member independently of his actual underwriting funds at Lloyd's is liable up to the last penny of his entire personal fortune outside Lloyd's for the due fulfilment of his underwriting obligations and thereafter his Policyholders have first call on his Deposit (pp. 19, 93.)

14. Until a Member's liabilities to his Policyholders have been paid in full, neither his Premium Trust Fund nor his Deposit can be attached by any other creditors. (pp. 99, 100.)

15. Over and above all the foregoing safeguards to Holders of Lloyd's policies there are

> (*a*) the Central Guarantee Fund, started in 1926, and now amounting to more than £1,750,000. (pp. 110, 112.)

and (*b*) a comprehensive system of Individual Guarantees aggregating several millions of pounds sterling as required by the Assurance Companies Act of 1909. (pp. 101, 112.)

16. The present financial structure of Lloyd's may be considered as dating from the voluntary adoption by Lloyd's of "the Audit" and the passing of the Lloyd's Section of the Assurance Companies Act of 1909. Since then the aggregate of claims paid to Lloyd's Policyholders is certainly far in excess of £800,000,000 and—notwithstanding three of the most severe tests of financial strength in History, viz. the two World Wars and the World Depression of the early 1930's—*no Holder of a Lloyd's policy making a bona fide claim has lost a penny as the result of the insolvency of a Lloyd's Underwriter.* (p. 96.)

17. Apart from its unassailable financial strength, probably the most striking feature about Lloyd's is the outstanding degree to which its system of working has engendered and developed initiative and originality amongst its Members—which characteristics, perhaps more than anything else, have contributed towards the remarkable success achieved by Lloyd's in meeting the ever changing and widening insurance requirements of the public. (pp. 40–42.)

18. In early days it was usual for every separate Lloyd's Underwriter to transact his business in person and he personally decided whether and on what terms he would engage in an insurance. If his underwriting ventures proved successful he alone took the profits—if unsuccessful the entire losses came out of his pocket. Every encouragement was thus afforded to personal initiative and independence—coupled with prudence. (p. 13.)

19. Nowadays at Lloyd's the actual work performed earlier by individual Underwriters for themselves is performed by a number of separate Underwriting

B

Agents, each conducting business for a Group (or Syndicate) made up of a number of Members. (pp. 19, 29, 30, 34.)

20. Each of these Underwriting Agents is, for all practical purposes, his own master free to transact business for his Group on whatever terms he chooses (subject, of course, to the Members in the Group individually conforming to the financial requirements of the British Government and the Committee). Thus the "individualism" which played such an important part in the early days of Lloyd's is equally or even more in evidence to-day. (pp. 40-42.)

21. Whilst the financial structure of a Group at Lloyd's is in no way like that of an Insurance Company, nevertheless at first sight there is a certain resemblance between such a Group and an ordinary Insurance Company working on very independent lines—similarly there is a certain resemblance between some of the duties of an Underwriting Agent for a Group at Lloyd's and those of the Manager of an ordinary Insurance Company. (p. 32.)

22. Practically every single existing type of Non-Marine Insurance, other than Life and Fire, was invented or first seriously practised at Lloyd's and it is probably safe to say that hardly a day passes without some novel departure in insurance conditions or practice being tried out and developed in the skilled competition which obtains between the many different Underwriting Agents at Lloyd's. (pp. 48, 69, 70.)

23. With but few exceptions none of the individual Members who comprise any Group takes any active part in the conduct of the underwriting business which is conducted for the Group by its Underwriting Agent and

so far as the Reader is concerned there is little, if any, need for him to think of the different Names which subscribe a Lloyd's Policy as being anything more than symbols of first-class security. (p. 31.)

24. The holder of a Policy issued by a first-class Insurance Company has no need to concern himself with the names of the Shareholders of that Company and similarly the holder of a Lloyd's Policy need not concern himself with the names of the Members of Lloyd's who subscribe it. (pp. 96, 109.)

25. The separate Members who comprise any Group operate purely as individuals responsible solely for their respective shares in any insurances undertaken by that Group. No kind of partnership exists between any of them and a Lloyd's Policy is so worded that it is a separate contract between the policyholder and each of the Names or Underwriters subscribing it. (pp. 19, 20, 30.)

26. Because of this it is sometimes thought that in the event of dispute it would be necessary to bring a separate Law Suit against each of the separate Underwriters. Although millions of Lloyd's Policies have been issued, so far as is known no such happening is on record. (p. 67.)

27. Since the terms and conditions of any Lloyd's Policy apply without variation to *all* the Underwriters subscribing it, any legal decision relating to any matter (such as liability for any claim) of common interest to these Underwriters would affect them all. Consequently, in the rare cases where in connection with a Lloyd's Policy a difficulty arises which can only be settled in a Court of Law, it is the practice for all the Underwriters concerned to agree that the result of a Test Action

brought against one of them will be binding on all. (p. 68.)

28. Underwriters at Lloyd's do not work direct with the public and insurances can be effected at Lloyd's only through duly authorised Lloyd's Brokers in London, of whom there are between 200 and 300, each of whom has to conform to rules laid down by the Committee of Lloyd's. Correspondents of different Lloyd's Brokers may be found throughout the World. (pp. 31, 34, 78.)

29. At numerous ports or places in different Countries the Corporation of Lloyd's has appointed what are officially termed "Lloyd's Agents," whose duties consist, for the greater part, in dealing with marine losses or claims and supplying shipping intelligence. Their general activities in no way resemble those of the ordinary Agent of an Insurance Company. The fact that a firm is a Correspondent of a Lloyd's Broker, through whom this firm is able to negotiate insurances at Lloyd's, does not in any way entitle the firm to style itself a Lloyd's Agent. (p. 76.)

30. Lloyd's Underwriters avoid many of the expenses which are incurred by most Insurance Companies because

> The Corporation of Lloyd's does not advertise nor does it solicit business and it very strongly discourages any kind of advertising on the part of any of its individual Members. (p. 72.)

> Generations of Underwriters and Underwriting Agents have been brought up in an atmosphere where success in selection of business depends on the exercise of individual judgment and experience rather than on the application of cut-and-dried

methods and elaborate formulæ. (pp. 37-42, 51.)

Every Member's business comes to him entirely through Lloyd's Brokers who themselves bear the costs —office premises and staffs, travelling, correspondence, cables, etc., etc.,—of securing and subsequently looking after this. (p. 43.)

31. The comparatively low overhead expenses of Lloyd's Underwriters are reflected in the favourable rates of premium which they are able to charge with consequent advantage to themselves and to their Policyholders. (pp. 41, 44.)

CHAPTER II

The Beginnings of Lloyd's

WHEN attempting to answer the question: "What really is Lloyd's?" it is very difficult to know where to start. In this book we are essentially dealing with the present and *not* with the past, but nevertheless in order to obtain an idea of what Lloyd's is *now*, it is necessary to refer very briefly to the manner in which Marine Insurance—on which Lloyd's was originally founded—was transacted about 250 years ago when were planted the seeds from which the present-day Lloyd's has grown. At the same time emphasis must be laid on the fact that what follows does not in any way purport to be a history of Lloyd's* nor does it attempt to tell of Lloyd's world-wide activities in connection with shipping matters.

It is quite clear that Marine Insurance was an established type of undertaking in England considerably earlier than the year 1600, but it is equally evident that in those days, and, indeed, for long afterwards, it was far from being a specialised business or profession. There seems little doubt that in the days of which we are speaking most Merchants and others who required Marine Insurance to protect their cargoes or vessels obtained this not from Companies or persons whose *primary* business was the granting of insurances but rather from individuals such as other Merchants who from time to time

---

* For such the Reader is recommended to that exhaustive and interesting volume entitled *A History of Lloyd's* compiled by Charles Wright and C. Ernest Fayle and published in 1928. Some of what is written in this present Outline is but a very brief and most inadequate synopsis of parts of the work in question. Another recent and very interesting book is *Lloyd's, A Historical Sketch*, by Ralph Straus.

accepted Insurance risks as a side-line to their main business.

In such circumstances it naturally happened frequently that the value of a cargo or vessel which had to be insured was very much greater than the amount which any one of these individual Insurers was prepared to hazard on a single venture. Thus it would often come about that an insurance was divided between a number of different individual Insurers but, of course, each of these separate Insurers was only responsible for the particular amount which he individually had agreed to hazard—in other words, the Owner of the cargo or vessel which was to be insured entered into a separate contract with each of the individuals who were granting him the insurance.

Although an Owner might thus have entered into separate contracts with a number of different individual Insurers, it would obviously have been unnecessarily cumbersome if, in connection with these contracts, all being on identical terms as to premium and conditions, each separate Insurer had been required to sign a separate Policy. Consequently, it was customary for the terms and conditions of the insurance to be set out on a form of Policy which was so worded that although it was but a single document it nevertheless constituted a number of separate contracts between the Owner on the one hand and on the other hand each of the different Insurers who signed the Policy "each for his own part and not one for another."

Each Insurer, when signing (or "subscribing") his name at the foot of the Policy, set against his name the particular amount which he had agreed to insure. From the practice of so signing their names at the foot of the Policies these Insurers came to be known as "Underwriters," whilst the Insurance business which they carried on came to be spoken of as "underwriting."

Now it will be readily appreciated that to people engaged in underwriting Marine Insurance it was in the olden days (as it still is) of great importance to have early news of occurrences or developments either at home or overseas which might affect their business. At the time with which we are dealing the telegraph and the telephone were, of course, unknown, the transport of letters was very slow and uncertain, newspapers worthy of the name did not exist, and items of news and reports of recent happenings were, for the greater part, disseminated by word of mouth.

There was thus a marked tendency for Owners of vessels, Sea Captains, Merchants and others in London who were interested in shipping matters, to foregather and exchange news since there was no other means of keeping in touch with current events affecting their interests.

In the absence of any official centre (such as the Exchanges or Bourses of modern times) it was natural that certain places came to be recognised as the rendezvous for persons having certain business interests in common and it was equally natural that many of these recognised places were places where refreshments could be obtained.

Such a place was a Coffee House kept by one Edward Lloyd, Coffee-Man, first in Tower Street whence in 1691 he moved to Lombard Street, where he died in 1713. To Lloyd's Coffee House came many Merchants and others particularly interested in shipping matters, and it seems clear that by 1710 it was looked on as an important centre for various persons interested in maritime matters, although it had not yet come to be associated with Insurance in particular.

However, specialisation was developing, the advent of the professional Underwriter was approaching, and it seems apparent that by about 1734 Lloyd's Coffee House was definitely an Insurance centre.

It was about this year that the proprietor of Lloyd's Coffee

LLOYD's LIST. N° 560.

FRIDAY, January 2. 1740.

THIS List, which was formerly publiſh'd once a Week, will now continue to be publiſh'd every *Tueſday* and *Friday*, with the Addition of the Stocks, Courſe of Exchange, &c.——Subſcriptions are taken in at Three Shillings per Quarter, at the Bar of *Lloyd's* Coffee-Houſe in *Lombard-Street*.

Such Gentlemen as are willing to encourage this Undertaking, ſhall have them carefully deliver'd according to their Directions.

London Exchanges on		Aids in the Exchequer	Given for	Paid off
Amſt. 34 11 a 10		18th 2 Shilling 1739	1000000	926800
Ditto Sight 34 7¼a8		18th 4 Ditto 1740	2000000	482600
Rott. 35 a 1		Malt—— 1739	750000	501014
Antw. 35 11 a 36		Salt—— 1734	1000000	910500
Hamb: 33 10 2Ua11 2¼				

Paris — 32¼				
Ditto at 2U 32¼		Gold in Coin - - - -	3 18 1	
Bourdeaux ⎱ 32¼		Ditto in Barrs - - -	3 18	
Uſance ⎰		Pillar large - - -	0 5 7 ¼	
Cadiz — 42¼		Ditto Small - -	0 5 6 ¼	
Madrid 42¼		Mexico large - -	0 5 7 ¼	
Bilboa 41¼		Ditto Small - -	0 5 6 ¼	
Leghorn 51¼		Silver in Barrs - - -	0 5 7 ¼	
Genoa 55				
Venice 51½		**Annuities**		
Lisbon 5 4¾25		14l. per Cent at 22½ Years Purchaſe		
Oporto 5 4¼		1704 to 1708 Incluſive 24½ ditto		
Dublin 8		3¼ per Cent. 1 per Cent. præm.		
		3 per Cent. 5¼ Diſc.		

Cochineal 20s 0d per. lb. Diſcount 00s per Cent.

Lottery 1710.

Prizes for 3 Years from *Michaelmas* laſt are in courſe of Payment
Blanks for 3 Years from *Michaelmas* laſt 1l. 10s *per* Set.

—Price of Stocks—	Wedneſday	Thurſday	Friday
Bank Stock - - - - -	138¼ a¼		138½
Eaſt India - - - - - - -		156	156a56¼
South Sea - - - - -	98¼		98½
Ditto Anuity Old	110¼a10	110⅞	110⅞
Ditto——— New	110¼a¼	110½	110½
3 per Cent. ⎱1726			99⅜
Annuity - ⎰1731			
Million Bank - - -	113	113	113
Equivalent - - - - - -	112	112	112
R. Aſſ. 100l paid in			
L: Aſſ. 13l paid in	10⅞	10¼	10⅞
7 per Cent Em. Loan	98	98	98
5 per Cent. Ditto	74⅞	74½	75
Bank Circulation	2l 10s 0d	2l 10s 0d	2l 10s 0d
Lottery Tickets	5l 16s 0d	5l 17s 0d	6l 00s 0d

India Transfer Books open the 19th of January
Royal Aſſurance the 20th of January
South Sea New Annuity the 22d of January, 3 per Cent Annuities the 21ſt and 22d of January
South Sea Stock the 4th of February
The 5 per Cent Emperor's Loan, ſells as above without the ſix Months Intereſt of 3 and a quarter per Cent, and 5 per Cent. part of the Principal to be paid of both, are now paying at the Bank
The India Dividend will be paid the 29th of January, South Sea New Annuities the 29th ditto, and the S. Sea Stock the 6th and 7th of February,
Navy and Victualling Bills to the 30th June laſt are in courſe of Payment.

—Intereſt per Cent	Wedneſday	Thurſday	Friday	
3 India Bonds new	79	80	80	⎱ Shill: ⎰ Præms
4 Salt Tallies	⅜ a ⅜	⅜ a ⅝	¼ a ⅜	

EARLIEST EXTANT COPY OF LLOYD'S LIST

Gravesend——	Arrived from
30 Dec. Draper, Leach	Dublin
Katherine, Roberts	Figuera
Globe, Harvey	Lisbon
Expedition, Major	Gibralter
1 Industry, Sheppardson	Virginia
Leostoff	arrived from
Swedish Liberty, Vischer	Stockholm
Harwich——	arrived from
Success, Hartley	Gottenburg
Liberpool——	—arrived from
Dove, Drinkwater	Virginia
Leopard, —— —	ditto
Bristol —— ——	arrived from
31 Elizabeth, Cheshire	Antigua
Penzance	Arrived from
Anne Sloop, Mitchel	Maderia
Falmouth ——	Arrived from
27 Cleve, Rice	London
	Sailed for
Mary Galley, Cross	Gibralter
Dartmouth——	Arrived from
28 Greenwich, ——	London
Paulker, ——	N.foundland
30 Port Merch. Wall.s	Lisbon
	Came in for
Mercurius, Waddle	Lisbon
Pool ——	Arrived from
27 Watfons Adv. Watson	Lisbon
Rainbow, Skolds	ditto
Patience, Bowles	ditto
29 Betsy, Addis	Carolina
31 Agnes & Mary, Pottle	N.foundland
Wm. & Thomas, Lander	London
Cowes	Arrived from
29 Brunswick, Payne	Carolina
Carter, Cork	Alderney
Nicholas, Hains	Cherburgh
	Came in for
St. Nicholas, Vesseur	Callais
Concordia, Trock	Hamburg
Helena, Guillaume	Carolina
Difpatch, Wallace	Dublin
Two Maries, Gordon	Southton
	Saild for
Neptune, Stevens	Holland
D. of Berwick, Basset	ditto
London, Bourleigh	ditto
Marygold, Joy	ditto
Southampton——	arrived from
30 Sarah, Withall	Oporto
Expedition Packet	Guernsey
	Sailedfor
Martler, Martin	Amsterdam
Portsmouth ——	Arrived from
	Came in for
30 Apollo, Brown	Jamaica
Britannia, Tremble	ditto
Enterprize, Wood	Barbadoes
Mahone, Stamper	Gibralter
Gould, Hudson	Carolina
Dover ——	arrived from
31 Carlille, Jefferson	Whitehaven

Eagle, Stavely	Biddiford
Mary & Ellen, Rush	Leverpool
——, Slade	ditto
Fidelia, Monkheufe	Dublin
Mary-Ann, Craigh	Limerick
——, Neman	Gotfenburg
Nancy, Tracy	Madeira
Downs —— —	Arrived from
30 K. of Portugal, Hughes	Lisbon
Algarve, Olding	Faro
St. John, Farrel	Antigua
31 Webster, Stevens	Cheshet
Halsey & Suttle, Salisbury	ditto
1 Marys Reign, Jervoise	Barbadoes
Wm. & Ann, Main	St. Kitts
Brittania, Farmer	New-York
	Remain for
Two Dutch Ships	EastIndia
A Dutch Ship	Guiney
London, Pipon	Gibralter
Concord, Spilman	Carolina
Ann, Watson	Maryland
Swallow, Hutchinson	Philadelphia
Praleda, Herbert	Cork
Minabilla, Blake	Lisbon
Ann, Ebsworthy	Guiney
Olliver, Pain	Gibralter
Naffau, Spilman	Falmouth
Hannah, Kilpatrick	Portsmouth
Paradox, Righton	St. Kitts

Winds at Deal.

30 SW 31 W 1 NW

Dublin —— ——	arrived from
Providence, Steward	London
Edw. & Mary, Littler	ditto
Eagle,	ditto
Cork ——	Arrived from
15 Martha, Purkefs	Southton
Jane & Betty, Jackson	Carolina
William, Higat	Isle of Man
Margaret, Robinson	Dublin
17 Hibernia, Comerford	Briftol
18 St. Louis, Evans	Bourdeaux
19 Richard, Crowley	Dublin
Swift, Denroach	Briftol
20 Succefs, Allen	Oftend
Mary, Phelan	Waterford
Mary & Betty, M'Goran	Leverpool
Succefs, Wadmore	Southton
21 Neftor, Moreshin	Hav
Diligence, Milican	Isle of Man
Henry, Richardson	Portsmouth
Margaret, Bryon	Bruges
Two Janes, Portivere	Dublin
3 Brothers, Webb	Briftol
	Sailed bound for
16 Kath. & Dorothy, Simmonds	Bourd.
18 Brereton, Hammond	Jamaica
19 Lyme Man.of War	a Cruize

THE TOP PARAGRAPH ON THE FACE INDICATES
THAT THIS WAS THE FIRST NUMBER OF LLOYD'S
LIST TO INCLUDE FINANCIAL AS WELL AS
SHIPPING INTELLIGENCE

House took the far reaching step of establishing and publishing a newspaper called *Lloyd's List* which, in its earlier days, was devoted exclusively to shipping intelligence. Although we may suppose that he had little more in mind than to provide a further amenity for the customers of his establishment, there seems little doubt that his venture proved a definite boon to the underwriting fraternity in general. This newspaper, which has been published without interruption ever since, is nowadays printed in the building occupied by the present-day Lloyd's, and is, apart from the official *London Gazette* published by the Government, the oldest surviving newspaper in London.

By 1750 the influence of the Underwriters frequenting Lloyd's Coffee House undoubtedly dominated the world of Marine Insurance, and 1760 saw the issue of the first *Register of Shipping*. That this important publication was issued not by the proprietor of Lloyd's Coffee House but by a "Society of Underwriters" at Lloyd's Coffee House seems to show that these Underwriters, whilst still trading as individuals "each for his own part and not one for another," were nevertheless, beginning to recognise the need for the formation of some central organisation to deal with matters affecting their mutual interests.

The recognition of this need took very practical form in 1771 when—the business carried on by the proprietors (as distinct from the frequenters) of the original Lloyd's Coffee House having in the meantime suffered many vicissitudes— there came an all-important change in the whole position. In that year seventy-nine Merchants, Underwriters and Brokers banded together and agreed to pay £100 each into a fund which was to be held in the names of a Committee and employed for the purpose of securing more suitable premises in which to conduct their business. Thus came into existence a definite body of individuals primarily concerned with underwriting and having premises which, though known as New Lloyd's Coffee House belonged to the Subscribers instead of to a Coffee-Man.

The new premises, when eventually secured, consisted of rooms in the Royal Exchange and, except for a short period when the Royal Exchange was being rebuilt after a fire, it was in this building that Lloyd's Underwriters carried on their business from that time up to 1928 when they moved to the premises in Leadenhall Street known as Lloyd's Building.

This band of seventy-nine individuals having taken the step of appointing a Committee for the purpose of securing their new premises, it was natural, after taking possession of these premises, that a Committee should still be maintained in order to deal with various questions arising out of the occupation of these premises and the business which the Subscribers carried on therein. In the course of years more and more powers were vested in the Committee which gradually came to acquire a position of very real importance, until it ultimately developed into what might be described as the governing body in the community of Subscribers by whom it was elected. At the same time it always was, and still is, a basic principle that the Committee must be very guarded in taking any action which might tend to restrict or interfere with the right possessed by every individual in this community to transact his own business in his own way.

The Committee played an active part in advancing and defending the interests of the Subscribers; amongst other matters it accumulated funds which it held for the common good and it established a chain of "Lloyd's Agents"* at various ports. Further, the running of the newspaper, *Lloyd's List*, which for some half a century had been a source of personal profit to others than the actual Subscribers for whose

* See page 76.

convenience it was provided, was eventually taken over by the Committee, which also played an important part in the establishment of a definite "Society of Lloyd's Register"* which deals with the classification of vessels and publishes the well-known *Lloyd's Register*.

Rules came into being regulating the classes of persons who, as Subscribers, might have access to the premises of New Lloyd's Coffee House and developing out of these rules different regulations were gradually evolved governing

Underwriting Members   —who alone were empowered to grant insurances.

Non-Underwriting Members—who had all the privileges of Underwriting Members except that they were not allowed to grant insurances.

Annual Subscribers   —consisting for the greater part of Brokers.

Substitutes   —chiefly clerks employed by different Underwriting Members and by different Brokers.

Associates   —being chiefly certain persons whose business brought them into frequent and close touch with different Members and Subscribers.

The making for the first time in 1843 of a differentiation between Members and Subscribers, and also various other happenings, increasingly tended to focus attention on the question of the security which was afforded to the holders of Policies signed by Members. However, those at Lloyd's who, as time went on, sought to bring in rules requiring Members

* Otherwise known as "Lloyd's Register of Shipping." See page 79.

to provide guarantees of their financial responsibility or to make deposits with the Committee did not by any means have things all their own way—they were doubtless accused of attempting to interfere with the sacred liberty of the individual—but notwithstanding this opposition it eventually became customary for the Committee, when electing new Members, to demand from them certain guarantees or deposits and in 1870 an actual rule was made requiring all new Members to put up a deposit of £3,000 on their election. Compared with present-day regulations this does not appear a very impressive figure but the bringing in of this rule had far-reaching consequences.

Important changes likewise came about from an incident in the same year which brought to light that, constituted as Lloyd's then was, its Members had not the power to expel one of their number whose conduct fell short of the standards of the community.

In order to correct this position the Committee and all the remaining Members decided to apply for an Act of Parliament which would enable the Members of Lloyd's to constitute themselves as a definite Society recognised by the Legislature, with statutory powers to make its own bye-laws, able to acquire for itself real as well as personal property and in a position to do all acts in its Corporate name.

The required Act of Incorporation was passed in 1871, and as a result of this Lloyd's became a legally recognised Society or Corporation, each Member of which, however, retained his right to carry on his own particular business in his own way, subject only to adherence to the bye-laws of the Corporation.*

* For the benefit of readers in Countries where the term "Corporation" is normally used in the sense of meaning merely an ordinary "Stock" or "Limited Liability" company or firm, it should here be explained that as applied to Lloyd's this term "Corporation" has for all practical purposes no other meaning than "Society" or "Association". In fact Lloyd's is very much in the nature of a club maintained by and for the benefit of its members and subscribers.

CHAPTER III

Lloyd's as a Corporation

EXCEPT that there have been changes consequent upon its growth and because of the necessity of adapting itself to ever-changing world conditions, the Lloyd's of to-day is very much the same as was Lloyd's at the time of its incorporation in 1871. Possibly the most striking changes have been

The growth of the system whereby the actual handling of a Member's underwriting business is done not by that Member himself but by a duly appointed Underwriting Agent who may simultaneously be carrying on similar business for a large number of different Members.

The development of Lloyd's as a market for Non-Marine Insurance.

The enactment of very stringent rules to ensure that absolute security is afforded to all holders of Lloyd's Policies.

Before we proceed to deal with these questions and other matters relating to Lloyd's of the present day, it is, perhaps, as well to refer once more to the two outstanding and basic principles which have ever governed the underwriting of insurances at Lloyd's, viz., firstly that although a number of Underwriters may subscribe a Lloyd's Policy, they all sign "each for his own part and not one for another," and secondly, that every Lloyd's Underwriter assumes *unlimited personal liability* for the insurances which he underwrites. It may at first sight seem strange that these two principles of individual but unlimited personal liability should have survived at Lloyd's to the present day when most large businesses are carried on by Limited Liability Companies, but it can safely be said that it is this very characteristic of "individualism" which, more than any other factor, has contributed to the growth and virility of Lloyd's.

It must be remembered that, in many respects, Lloyd's is still what it was when Lloyd's Coffee House was merely a place where various Bankers, Merchants and Traders were free to meet and transact whatever business they individually considered desirable. They were not governed by hard-and-fast rules, but each was his own master, responsible only to himself—if an enterprising Underwriter at Lloyd's conceived some new idea in regard to Insurance, he was free to make the experiment of putting it to a practical test, being fully aware, however, that in so doing he was risking no one's money but his own. In this state of affairs initiative was engendered and encouraged to a degree which seldom, if ever, could have been attained had these old time individual Underwriters been the servants of a Company to which they, as employees, were accountable for their actions.

It is true that in earlier days before Lloyd's became a Corporation with power to make and enforce its own bye-laws this characteristic of individual freedom of action was not without its weaknesses. For example, due in part to the entire absence until some time after the incorporation of Lloyd's in 1871 of any adequate arrangements for securing that in-dividual Underwriters conducted their business at Lloyd's on a financially sound basis, there undoubtedly were instances where holders of Lloyd's policies were unable to recover claims in full by reason of the failure of one or more of these Underwriters. It must, however, be remembered that during

JN the Name of God, Amen. *Fermin & c Tasker Croft & Co*

as well in *their* own Name, as for and in the Name and Names of all and every other Person or Persons *to* whom the same doth, may, or shall appertain, in Part or in All, doth make *Assurance,* and *them,* and every of them to be Insured, lost or not lost, at and from

Liverpool to the Coast of Africa, during her stay & trade there and at & from thence to her port or ports of discharge in the Island of Cuba

Upon any Kind of Goods and Merchandizes, and also upon the Body, Tackle, Apparel, Ordnance, Munition, Artillery, Boat, and other Furniture, of and in the good Ship or Vessel called the

Gustavus &c

whereof is Master, under God, for this present Voyage, *William De Freine*
or whosoever else shall go for Master in the said Ship, or by whatsoever other Name or Names the same Ship, or the Master thereof, is or shall be named or called; beginning the Adventure upon the said Goods and Merchandizes from the Loading thereof aboard the said Ship

upon the said Ship, &c. *at & from Liverpool & Africa*
and *it* shall continue and endure, during her Abode there, upon the said Ship, &c. And further, until the said Ship, with all her Ordnance, Tackle, Apparel, &c. and Goods and Merchandizes whatsoever shall be arrived at *Africa and have sail or ports of discharge*
upon the said Ship, &c. until she hath moor'd at Anchor Twenty-four Hours in good Safety; and upon the Goods and Merchandizes, until the same be there discharged and safely landed. And it shall be lawful for the said Ship, &c. in this Voyage, to proceed and sail to and touch and stay at any Ports or Places whatsoever

without Prejudice to this Insurance. The said Ship, &c. Goods and Merchandizes, &c. for so much as concerns the Assureds, by Agreement between the Assureds and Assurers in this Policy are and shall be valued at

In case of collision, or a declaration of her being carried into port to be deemed a sufficient document to recover the loss

Touching the Adventures and Perils which we the Assurers are contented to bear, and do take upon us in this Voyage; they are of the Seas, Men of War, Fire, Enemies, Pirates, Rovers, Thieves, Jettizons, Letters of Mart and Counter Mart, Surprizals, Takings at Sea, Arrests, Restraints and Detainments of all Kings, Princes and People, of what Nation, Condition or Quality soever; Barretry of the Master and Mariners, and of all other Perils, Losses and Misfortunes, that have or shall come to the Hurt, Detriment or Damage of the said Goods and Merchandizes and Ship, &c. or any Part thereof. And in Case of any Loss or Misfortune, it shall be lawful to the Assureds, their Factors, Servants and Assigns, to sue, labour and travel for, in and about the Defence, Safeguard and Recovery of the said Goods and Merchandizes and Ship, &c. or any Part thereof, without Prejudice to this Insurance; to the Charges whereof we the Assurers will contribute each one according to the Rate and Quantity of his Sum herein Assured. And it is agreed by us the Insurers, that this Writing or Policy of Assurance shall be of as much Force and Effect as the surest Writing or Policy of Assurance heretofore made in Lombard-street, or in the Royal-Exchange, or elsewhere in London. And so we the Assurers are contented, and do hereby promise and bind ourselves, each one for his own Part, our Heirs, Executors, and Goods, to the Assureds, their Executors, Administrators, and Assigns, for the true Performance of the Premises, confessing ourselves paid the Consideration due unto us for this Assurance by the Assured   at and after the

Rate of *Twenty Guineas p Cent*

In Witness whereof we the Assurers have subscribed our Names and Sums Assured in London.

N. B. Corn, Fish, Salt, Fruit, Flour and Seed, are warranted free from Average, unless general, or the Ship be stranded.—Sugar, Tobacco, Hemp, Flax, Hides and Skins, are warranted free from Average, under Five Pounds per Cent. and all other Goods, also the Ship and Freight, are warranted free of Average under Three Pounds per Cent. unless general, or the Ship be stranded.

On Ship valued at £3500
Goods as shall be hereafter specified and valued
The Slaves valued at £45 each

A LLOYD'S POLICY ON SLAVES, 1794

This Policy vividly illustrates how ideas have changed since the days when it was issued.

One may assume that then none of the parties to it had any scruples about entering into an insurance—the Policy for which, moreover, started with the pious phrase 𝕴𝖓 𝖙𝖍𝖊 𝕹𝖆𝖒𝖊 𝖔𝖋 𝕲𝖔𝖉, 𝕬𝖒𝖊𝖓—relating to "slaves valued at £45 each."

Further, according to the conditions of the Policy, if in an insurrection less than five percent of the slaves were killed, this did not constitute a claim. Accordingly, it would seem that on a vessel carrying slaves such episodes as insurrections on the part of the "cargo" were regarded as more or less normal happenings, so that one in which less than five percent were killed was looked upon merely as an ordinary "trade risk."

that earlier epoch and also later, bankruptcies elsewhere in the Insurance Market must have caused infinitely greater losses to the public.

At all events, the fact that since its beginning and especially during more modern times the public has, to an ever-growing degree, made use of the Insurance facilities afforded by Lloyd's is striking evidence that these few earlier failures did little real harm to Lloyd's as a whole and is equally striking evidence of the inherent soundness of the methods employed by Underwriters in conducting their business at Lloyd's.

Although, with the passing of time and the enactment of laws to ensure that Companies and their finances are properly managed, there are now a great number of Insurance Companies which are, with every right, world famed, it is certain that they could never fulfil the same functions as Lloyd's, where every Underwriter, although nowadays having to conform to rules which afford his policy-holders the highest degree of security, still acts "each for his own part and not one for another," and where, in consequence, the fullest possible encouragement and opportunity is given to those who are blessed with the capacity to originate new ideas or who have the courage to put these to a practical test at their own risk.

We have already shown how from an undefined community of individuals interested in maritime matters there gradually developed a definitely organised society of individual Underwriters who as a body comprise the "Corporation of Lloyd's," and from what has been written it will also be seen that Lloyd's is in no way an "Insurance Company" in the generally accepted sense. Amongst the public a great deal of misconception exists in regard to this particular point, andno one will ever be able to grasp how Lloyd's operates unless this fact is always kept in mind.

The analogy is in no way exact, but just as the Stock

Exchange is a place where stocks and shares can be bought and sold, so, in a manner of speaking, is Lloyd's a place where insurances can be bought and sold—with, of course, this difference that in the case of Lloyd's the public only buys (and does not sell) insurance.

In the case of the Stock Exchange anyone of the general public who wishes to buy some particular shares does not buy these from the Stock Exchange itself, but employs a Stock-broker to buy the shares from some member of the Stock Exchange who is prepared to sell the desired sharès. Similarly anyone of the general public who wishes to effect an insurance with Lloyd's Underwriters (or in other words buy an insurance from Lloyd's Underwriters) does not get this insurance from the entity known as Lloyd's—instead he has to instruct a Lloyd's Broker to obtain for him an insurance of the required type from whatever Underwriting Members of Lloyd's are prepared to provide him with (i.e. sell to him) the required form of insurance.

Therefore, it must always be remembered that Lloyd's, i.e. the Corporation of Lloyd's, does not itself grant insurances or undertake any underwriting business, and that a "Lloyd's Policy"accordingly means a policy issued and subscribed by certain individual Members of Lloyd's, who, of course, have to conform to the rules and regulations of the Corporation of which they are members.   −

The Corporation, as such, owns property* and funds which it administers for the benefit of its individual Members and deals generally with matters affecting the interests of Members as a whole. This work is carried out by the Committee of Lloyd's with the help of the Corporation's permanent staff.

* In 1925 when the Committee of Lloyd's decided that the time had come for Lloyd's to have a building of its own, it was arranged that for certain business reasons the new building should belong to a Company which was formed under the title of Lloyd's Building Ltd. This Company, Lloyd's Building Ltd., is controlled by and for all practical purposes can be considered as the property of the Corporation of Lloyd's.

Of the twelve Underwriting Members of Lloyd's who comprise the Committee three retire annually and are not eligible for re-election until after an interval of a year. The Chairman and Deputy Chairman are elected every year by the Members of the Committee from amongst themselves and hold office for twelve months.

Besides the actual Members of Lloyd's who as a body constitute the Corporation of Lloyd's there are many other individuals and firms who are officially entitled to describe themselves as being "at Lloyd's" and arising out of this it has come about that the term "Lloyd's" is often used in a colloquial and wider sense as embracing all the different parties who work at Lloyd's. A summary of these has been given earlier,* but the following amplification may be of interest to some Readers:

Members.

These are of two kinds, viz. Underwriting Members and Non-Underwriting Members.† It is of these Members, Underwriting and Non-Underwriting, that the Corporation of Lloyd's is composed and it is only Members who are allowed to be present or vote at meetings of the Corporation.

Only Underwriting Members are permitted to carry on the business of underwriting, that is to say, the business of entering into contracts of Insurance and signing Lloyd's Policies. They, of course, all have access to the premises which are maintained by the Corporation and to any information, confidential or otherwise, which is collected and published for the benefit of Members.

Underwriting Members in turn fall into two categories. Firstly, those who themselves actually and in person conduct their underwriting business, so deciding for themselves what

* See page 17.

† The Committee as a very special mark of honour have on rare occasions since 1800 elected as Honorary Members certain individuals who have performed some particularly notable services which have been of benefit to Lloyd's or to their country.

insurances they will accept or decline, and secondly, those who employ an Underwriting Agent to conduct business on their behalf. A Member who conducts his own business and thus falls into the first category may act, and in fact generally does act, at the same time as Agent for a Member or group of Members falling within the second category.

Non-Underwriting Members have exactly the same privileges as Underwriting Members except that they may not carry on the business of underwriting and signing Lloyd's Policies.

Any individual who has been elected as a Member, whether Underwriting or Non-Underwriting, is also entitled to carry on business as an Insurance Broker at Lloyd's provided he conforms to certain rules laid down by the Committee. Naturally an Underwriting Member who both underwrites insurances and also acts as an Insurance Broker is required to keep these two sides of his business absolutely separate and distinct.

Annual Subscribers.

For the greater part these consist of persons who, being neither Underwriting nor Non-Underwriting Members, are nevertheless working as Lloyd's Brokers. The business of a Lloyd's Broker may be carried on either by an individual working for his own account with unlimited liability, or by two or more individuals working as an ordinary partnership with unlimited liability, or by a firm which has registered itself as a Limited Liability Company. In the case of a brokerage business being carried on by an individual or by a group of individuals working in partnership, the individual or one of the partners must be either an Underwriting or Non-Underwriting Member or an Annual Subscriber, whilst in the case of a brokerage business carried on by a Limited Liability Company one of the directors must be similarly qualified and the Company itself must be an Annual Subscriber.

Amongst the Subscribers are also to be found all the large British Marine Insurance Companies and many important British, Colonial and Foreign Shipping Companies. It must, however, be emphasised that these Insurance Companies and

Shipping Companies* do not possess the privilege of actually working "at Lloyd's" but since they and Lloyd's have many interests in common it is to the advantage of all parties that they should be in close touch with Lloyd's.

Associates.

These are not very numerous and consist of certain individuals such as Claims Adjusters, Lawyers, and Accountants who, although not directly engaged in Insurance, have close relations with Lloyd's or with its Members or Subscribers and so find it advantageous to have access to Lloyd's premises.

Substitutes.

These act as the representatives of individual Members or Subscribers who pay the Committee an annual subscription in respect of each person who is authorised by the Committee to act as a Substitute. Substitutes have access to the premises in which the business of Lloyd's is carried on, where they are entitled to work on behalf of the particular Members or Subscribers for whom they are acting as Substitutes. Naturally some of the Substitutes, of which there are a large number, occupy important and responsible positions—in fact, most of the individual Members and Annual Subscribers who are actively and personally engaged in business at Lloyd's have themselves at some time or other been Substitutes to earlier Members or Subscribers.

Before any person can become a Member (Underwriting or Non-Underwriting), Subscriber or Associate he must be elected by the Committee and on his election he is required to pay an entrance fee. These entrance fees and the annual subscriptions paid by such persons or on behalf of Substitutes represent annually a large sum and form a very valuable contribution towards the heavy expenses which are incurred

* As a side-line to their main business one or two Shipping Companies carry on an Insurance Brokerage business at Lloyd's.

by the Committee in the interests of Lloyd's Members and Subscribers.

The task of the Committee is certainly no easy one. For the benefit of any community there must of necessity be certain rules and regulations governing the individual, but on the other hand an excess of rules and regulations undoubtedly tends to hamper personal initiative and enterprise. The Committee is thus in the very difficult position of having to work "for the greatest good of the greatest number" out of a large community which for its successful progress depends primarily on the individual's right and power to exercise his own judgment and to act "each for his own part and not one for another." This right to independence and freedom of action is most jealously guarded by every Member of Lloyd's and, unless clearly recognised as being of undoubted benefit to the community as a whole, strenuous opposition has always been shown to the bringing in of any measures which might tend to curtail the individual's freedom of action.

The Committee is undoubtedly a very important force at Lloyd's but the power which it wields is exercised not so much by virtue of any defined rules and regulations or bye-laws as by the maintenance of various "Unwritten Laws" which play an all important part in the carrying on of business at Lloyd's.

Such actual rules and regulations as govern Members and Subscribers relate for the greater part to the arrangements designed to ensure that all holders of Lloyd's Policies have absolute security—apart from these, definitely laid down rules and regulations are surprisingly few in number.

The Committee has no kind of jurisdiction or control over the selection of business or the fixing of rates or conditions. Such matters are solely the concern of the individual Members, all of whom are entirely free to transact any type of business (except Financial Guarantees which may only be undertaken within certain strict limitations) on whatever terms they like subject, of course, to compliance with the Laws of the Country.* The Committee, however, can and does exercise very strict control over the volume of business which any individual Member transacts, the object of this being to ensure that no Member is over-trading and that he will always be in a position to meet his liabilities as an Underwriter. This aspect of the Committee's activities is dealt with at greater length later on† when outlining the nature of the security which is afforded to the Holders of Lloyd's Policies.

---

* Life Assurance in its usually accepted sense is not transacted generally at Lloyd's. At the same time it is perfectly open to any Underwriting Member to engage in this provided that he conforms to the Statutory Regulations which the British Government imposes on all persons carrying on such business. A limited number of Members do in fact conform to these Regulations but their operations are confined to certain very restricted types of Life Assurance.

† See Chapter X.

CHAPTER IV

Generally Explaining how Business is Transacted at Lloyd's

THERE is no doubt that the confusion which exists in the minds of many persons regarding the manner in which business is conducted at Lloyd's is enhanced by the rather loose manner in which the term "Underwriter" is employed. As has already been explained, it was customary in early days for each of the individuals who accepted a share of an insurance to sign his name at the bottom of the Policy, setting against his name the amount for which he personally had accepted liability. The different individuals who thus signed a Policy were described in it as "the Underwriters." At times it happened that the individual who was thus acting as an Underwriter did not himself personally conduct his underwriting activities, but employed an Agent to do this business for him. In such cases the Agent was authorised to sign Policies in the name of his Principal who, of course, was the actual Underwriter although he personally had not selected the insurance nor carried out the physical act of "underwriting" the insurance.

Thus there existed the Underwriter who personally carried on his own underwriting business and who himself signed his own name at the foot of Policies, while at the same time there was the Underwriting Agent who underwrote *for* another individual, the name of this latter individual being signed on the Policy as the Underwriter. As time went on the practice of employing an Underwriting Agent became more and more general, and nowadays by far the greater part of the underwriting which is carried on at Lloyd's is conducted by Agents.*

The Agent who in this way carries on business for someone else is, of course, really an "Underwriting Agent," but from the fact that it is he who is carrying out the specialised "work" involved in underwriting (albeit for his Principal) he very often is colloquially but incorrectly referred to as "the Underwriter." Thus when, as frequently happens in conversation or correspondence, reference is made to "the Underwriters" it is often difficult to distinguish whether the individuals referred to are the Underwriting Members whose actual names appear on a policy or the Underwriting Agents who act for these Underwriting Members.

By reason of this prevalent and rather misleading custom of employing the expression "Underwriters" when speaking of persons who really are Underwriting Agents, there is much to be said for the practice which is equally prevalent of using the term "Names" when speaking of the actual Underwriters whose names appear on the Policy. Accordingly, in the present Outline from this point onwards no further use will be made of the term "Underwriter" but the terms

"Name" or "Underwriting Member" or "Member" or "Lloyd's Underwriter" will always be employed as meaning an Underwriting Member of Lloyd's who (either personally or through an Underwriting Agent) accepts insurances and whose name and respective share of an insurance appears on a Policy.

and "Agent" or "Underwriting Agent" will always be employed as meaning the individual who is appointed by one or more Names to conduct the business of underwriting on behalf of the Name or Names.

* As explained in Chapter VII, an Underwriting Agent may be either an individual or a firm, but in order to avoid confusion at this stage it is proposed for the present to refer to an Underwriting Agent as if he were an individual only.

Although *originally* it was the practice for all Names to work entirely independently of each other, it is nowadays far more usual to find that the work is carried on by an Agent acting for a number of separate Names. In such cases it is customary, as a matter of convenience, for the different Names for which an Agent works to be formed into what is known as a Group or Syndicate. Where an Agent thus works for a Syndicate each of the Names concerned takes a definite pre-arranged share of every insurance which is accepted by the Agent on behalf of this Syndicate or Group, but it is important to remember that this does not in any way constitute any kind of partnership between the different Names in the Group—on the contrary, each Name is solely responsible for his particular share of the insurance in exactly the same way as if he had individually signed the Policy for a stated amount.

Some of these Groups consist of but a few, say less than half a dozen, Names but it is more usual to find Groups comprising from ten to thirty Names, whilst a few are very much larger, being made up of about eighty or more Names.

At the present time, 1947, there are some 2,300 Underwriting Members of Lloyd's (as compared with about 400 when the actual Corporation of Lloyd's came into being in 1871) most of whom transact both Marine and Non-Marine business. In earlier days, when only a limited volume of Non-Marine Insurance was handled at Lloyd's, it was usual for a Name who was carrying on his business through an Agent to empower this Agent to underwrite all classes of business for him, but the increasing complexities and striking growth of business during the present century have made specialisation more and more necessary. Consequently, with but few exceptions, any given Group primarily transacts either Marine *or* Non-Marine business so that those Underwriting Members who engage in both types are usually to be found as Names in two separate Groups, one writing Marine risks and the other writing Non-Marine risks.*

Usually, but not invariably, the Underwriting Agent for a Group of Names is himself a Name in the Syndicate for which he underwrites and he may quite likely also be a Name in another Syndicate which is underwritten for by a separate Agent who specialises in a different kind of business. For instance, if an individual were acting as the Marine Underwriting Agent for a Group in which he himself is a Name, as likely as not he will appoint someone else to be his Non-Marine Underwriting Agent and he will accordingly appear as one of the Names in the Non-Marine Group for which this separate Non-Marine Underwriting Agent acts.

Although an individual who is an Underwriting Member of Lloyd's may, of course, carry on some other occupation which is quite distinct from his business at Lloyd's, nevertheless the underwriting business which he (either personally or through his Underwriting Agent) as a Member of Lloyd's transacts with the Public may only be conducted through firms or persons who are duly authorised Lloyd's Brokers. Hence it follows that insurances can only be effected at Lloyd's through a duly authorised Lloyd's Broker.

From what has already been written it will be seen that so far as the public is concerned the Names on a Policy are little more than symbols of security† and as Names they, with but a few exceptions, do not take any active part in the handling of the business. The active parties in the handling of business at Lloyd's are, on the one hand the various Underwriting Agents, and on the other the many firms of duly authorised Lloyd's Brokers.

* Underwriting Members, on being elected, are required to give an undertaking that they will only employ one Agent to conduct Marine Underwriting and one Agent to conduct general Non-Marine underwriting. This restriction was not introduced in its present form until 1927.

† This important question of security is fully dealt with in Chapter X.

If one seeks for a point of similarity between the manner of placing business with ordinary Insurance Companies and the manner of placing business at Lloyd's, it might perhaps be permissible for a moment to think of the numerous separate Underwriting Agents at Lloyd's as roughly corresponding to the Managers of various different Insurance Companies, each of which, although operating independently of the others, conformed to certain very strict standards of security laid down by some central organisation. Actually, of course, any such resemblance is only superficial—and in any case there is the vital difference that the Manager of an Insurance Company is restricted to carrying out the underwriting policy laid down by his Board of Directors, whereas an Underwriting Agent at Lloyd's is entirely his own master in regard to the selection of business and if he wishes to branch out into new fields he is perfectly free to do so so long as the Names in his Group conform to the financial requirements of the British Government and the Committee of Lloyd's.

Before considering the actual procedure which is adopted when placing insurances at Lloyd's it is necessary to have some mental picture of Lloyd's premises.

The most important feature of the building in Leadenhall Street which is now occupied by Lloyd's is the Underwriting Room—ordinarily spoken of merely as "the Room." This is a vast hall containing a large number of desks arranged in rows and separated by gangways. These desks—which by an old custom are almost invariably referred to as "Boxes" —are allotted to different Underwriting Agents. These Boxes form an interesting link with the past in that their general design still conforms to that of the old-fashioned tables and benches which were in use in the days of the early Lloyd's Coffee House.

Elsewhere in the building are the offices of the Corporation's

A PORTION OF "THE ROOM"

large permanent staff which, under the direction of the Committee, deals with the great amount of administrative and routine detail with which the Committee has to concern itself on behalf of Lloyd's as a whole.* In addition, there are the various Committee, Reading and Reference Rooms, the Library, a Restaurant (which still goes by the name of "the Captains' Room," dating from the days of Lloyd's Coffee House), a Printing Establishment and many offices leased to different concerns who for business reasons wish to be in close proximity to "the Room."

At their different Underwriting Boxes in the Room sit the different Agents and their Deputies ready to discuss business with Brokers or Brokers' representatives—these latter spending the greater part of their time in the Room going to and from or waiting at different Underwriting Boxes to discuss their business with different Underwriting Agents.

Naturally in the Room itself there is nothing like the necessary accommodation for the whole of the staffs— the individuals comprising which in the aggregate number some thousands—of all the different Underwriting Agents and Lloyd's Brokers who frequent it. Some of these have their staffs in the same building in separate offices which they lease from the Corporation of Lloyd's, but the majority have their offices in other buildings in the neighbourhood.

The Underwriting Boxes vary in size, some having but two seats whilst others have eight or even more seats. These latter are, for the most part, occupied by Agents for some of the larger and more important Groups which transact a large volume of business, possibly of a very varied nature, the selection and handling of which an Agent in part delegates

---

* As examples of the routine details may be cited such matters as the collection of shipping and other intelligence, the publication of Lloyd's List, the checking and signing of policies on behalf of Members, the investigation of figures relating to Members' underwriting activities as required for the "the Audit" and other purposes, etc., etc.

to a number of different Deputies, each of whom often specialises in some particular branch of the business. In any case, apart from those Deputies whom an Agent may employ for any special purpose, it is necessary that he should have at least one Deputy who can deal with business in his absence. Many of these Deputies are, of course, very able and experienced men and many of them in due course themselves become Underwriting Agents employing their own Deputies.

The active Agents, i.e., those individuals who personally sit in their Underwriting Boxes and there conduct the business of underwriting for the Groups of Names which they represent are now about 150 in number, of which some specialise in Marine underwriting and some in Non-Marine underwriting. Only a few active Agents are general writers of both Marine and Non-Marine business.

The fact that Underwriting Members of Lloyd's may not deal direct with the public but only with Lloyd's Brokers means in effect that Lloyd's Brokers are intermediaries between the Underwriting Members of Lloyd's and those members of the public who wish to arrange their Insurances at Lloyd's. However, although a Lloyd's Broker thus acts as an intermediary, it must always be borne in mind that he is essentially the servant of his Clients and is *not* the agent for the Names (or their Underwriting Agents) with whom he places insurances for his Clients. Not only does the Marine Insurance Act of 1906 make it quite clear that as regards Marine Insurance a Broker is legally the agent of his Clients (and not the agent of the Insurers), but in any case it is self-evident that a Broker must, in his own interests, give the best possible service that he can to his Clients, since it is only by obtaining for his Clients better value for money than they could secure without his services that he can hope to build up and retain his business.

Persons unacquainted with the procedure at Lloyd's not infrequently think that each different firm of Brokers deals only with certain particular Groups, but this is an entirely erroneous idea,* and it should here be emphasised that every Lloyd's Broker is free to do business with any and all of the different Underwriting Agents at Lloyd's. Indeed, it is one of the unwritten laws at Lloyd's that an Underwriting Agent must be entirely impartial and give absolute equality of treatment to all the different Brokers with whom he does business.

While all Lloyd's Brokers may thus be deemed to have equal opportunities for the handling of business and while every Broker must in his own interests aim at being able to give efficient service to his Clients in regard to any and all types of insurance, there is perhaps rather a tendency for certain Brokers to become especially associated with certain kinds of business or to build up a clientèle from amongst certain sections of the public.

At the present time, 1947, there are about 230 different firms of Lloyd's Brokers, the individual staffs of which vary from but a few employees up to 200 or 300 or even more, of which, however, by far the greater number never go to Lloyd's itself but work entirely in the offices of their respective firms. Naturally, just as there are variations in the numbers of staff employed by different Brokers, so there are marked differences in the volume of business transacted by different firms, but the Reader most certainly must not assume that because one firm is smaller than another it is necessarily less capable. Manifestly in no profession can the mere numbers of a firm's staff or the size of its business be considered as an infallible index to the firm's efficiency—at Lloyd's as in all business circles every large firm of to-day began in a much smaller way.

* This subject is further referred to in Chapter VII.

An important fact which is more fully referred to later*
but which should be mentioned here is that while Lloyd's
Underwriters may only accept business from duly authorised
Lloyd's Brokers, a Lloyd's Broker is in no way restricted to
doing business only with Lloyd's Underwriters but is perfectly
free also to work with any Insurance Companies he chooses.
Many firms of Lloyd's Brokers make extensive use of Insurance
Companies and there is no doubt that a very large amount
of business, both Marine and Non-Marine, is arranged by
Lloyd's Brokers with Insurance Companies (as distinct from
Lloyd's Underwriters). Probably every thoughtful Reader
will be of the opinion that it is to the unquestioned benefit
of the public that Lloyd's Brokers have this freedom of action.

* See page 84.

CHAPTER V

Generally Describing the Activities of Underwriting Agents and of Lloyd's Brokers

THE primary activities of an Underwriting Agent naturally consist of the selection of the insurances which he undertakes and the examination of claims, and every Agent employs one or more Deputies or Assistants who, when he is absent or engaged, have authority to deal with these sides of his business. The selection of his business by an Underwriting Agent is, for the greater part, carried out by him in his Box at Lloyd's where he sits ready to look into and discuss the different propositions which different Brokers wish to put before him. The conditions under which he works at his Box, particularly if he is in considerable demand, are frequently trying and arduous in the extreme since as often as not, while surrounded by quite a crowd and in the far from peaceful atmosphere of the Room, he has to arrive at quick decisions regarding the host of widely differing propositions which in rapid turn are put before him. This means that in the space of perhaps but a few minutes he may have to switch his thoughts and attention from one to another of a number of cases involving the most diverse types of insurance in connection with hazards and properties of the most diverse nature in utterly different situations and subject to entirely different circumstances. It will readily be understood that conditions such as these are not suited for the application of what may be termed very scientific methods of underwriting but rather that they definitely encourage the development of something in the nature of an "underwriting instinct."

Naturally in the ranks of both Marine and Non-Marine Agents at Lloyd's there are certain individuals who have come to be looked upon by many of their fellow Agents as recognised authorities on particular forms of Insurance. These Agents are said to be "leaders" for those kinds of business, and a Broker who wishes to place an insurance of the type in question will, in most cases, endeavour to get one of these leaders to take a share of the insurance, or in other words to "lead" the insurance. If the Broker succeeds in obtaining a "lead" from an Underwriting Agent who is recognised as an expert by certain of his fellow Agents, naturally the "lead" thus obtained will influence some of these fellow Agents towards accepting shares of the insurance for account of the Groups for which they underwrite.

Of course, in some cases, it happens that an Agent who ranks as a leader for certain kinds of insurances may be but one of the rank and file as regards many other types and, again, there are Agents, some of them eminently successful, who never set out to be leaders but are quite content to be followers.

By far the greater portion of the enormous volume of business which is arranged annually at Lloyd's consists of insurances to which no recognised scales of rates are applicable and it may indeed be said that as regards many forms of Insurance the fixing of rates is, to no small degree, a matter of guesswork, such guesswork, however, being backed by a large measure of experience and common sense. Of course some types of Insurance lend themselves far more readily than do others to the application of really scientific methods—a notable example being Life Assurance, the rates of premium for which are based on extraordinarily detailed *past* records which enable Actuaries to calculate future claims ratios with a very high degree of accuracy.

Obviously, nothing like such scientific methods can be employed in the handling of many other forms of Insurance, particularly Marine Insurance—on which it must be remembered the business of Lloyd's was originally founded.

Although nowadays the writing of Non-Marine insurances at Lloyd's is for the greater part conducted by Agents who specialise in this branch of business, nevertheless they have grown up and worked in an atmosphere and surroundings impregnated with the traditions and customs appertaining to the handling of Marine Insurance. Consequently it is not surprising to find that at Lloyd's both Marine and Non-Marine Underwriting Agents have much in common in their methods of approach to business.

A Marine Underwriting Agent may take great trouble to compile records and analyses of the results of different kinds of Marine insurances which he has written for the past twenty or thirty years, but quite apart from the incalculable factor of weather vagaries, it is obvious that because of the ever-changing conditions of commerce and continuous developments in methods of transport, these records can have little scientific value although they serve as a rough, albeit very useful, guide to what may be anticipated from month to month at the present time.

Very much the same state of affairs exists as regards an Underwriting Agent engaged in writing general Non-Marine insurances. In our present-day civilisation there are continuously being introduced so many new factors, the ultimate effects of which can only be a matter of conjecture, that no *past* records which may be available can—at all events for many types of business—be regarded as in any way providing

D

a mathematically exact guide to the future course of events.*

When, as at Lloyd's, every Underwriting Agent is free to weigh up for himself the pros and cons of any insurance which he is considering, he will naturally pay attention to any statistics which are available—but statistics *as such* do not play the vital part at Lloyd's that they do with other important Insurance Organisations conducting their business on the basis of fixed scales of rates more or less arbitrarily based on statistics.

Thus it comes about that the methods employed by the average Non-Marine Underwriting Agent in carrying on and selecting business at Lloyd's may, at first sight, appear to be very unorthodox or even crude to anyone who is accustomed to the more "systemized" methods of other Insurance Organisations. However when, as at Lloyd's, the whole of this work is done in person by trained Underwriting Agents each of whom, although styled an Agent, has in effect all the powers of a Principal with all freedom to exercise his own personal judgment, there is obviously far less need for any system of rigid rates and conditions than there is in the case of some other Insurance Organisations, the selection of business for which is entrusted to numerous different employees and representatives who, for many reasons, must necessarily be governed by fairly rigid rules and formulæ precluding the exercise of more than a very limited degree of individual judgment.

A further advantage which arises in the Lloyd's system of underwriting on the basis of individual judgment rather than on a basis which sets out to be highly systemized is that the former method does not involve Underwriting Agents and their Names in anything like such heavy overhead charges

* It is reported that a certain very able Marine Underwriting Agent, on being asked what particular characteristic above all contributed towards success in underwriting at Lloyd's, replied "the ability to form a correct conclusion from inadequate premises."

and expenses as are entailed under any system which, being primarily based on statistics, requires the employment of large staffs to cope with the vast amount of detail which must necessarily be referred to and recorded.

The economies thus effected (as compared with the cost of working on a more statistical basis) allow a certain financial margin out of which can be met the possibly higher claims ratio which may result from adopting somewhat elastic rather than very scientific methods.

Although what may be described as "scientific" methods are seldom employed by Underwriting Agents when considering what rates and conditions to apply to any particular case, it must not be thought that they arrive at their decisions in a purely fortuitous way. Most Agents have had many years personal experience at Lloyd's, and when considering any given case, unless this is of a very out-of-the-way type, an Agent will probably be able to recall or discover from his records a number of other cases which he has written in the past and which have certain characteristics more or less in common with the case which is under consideration. He will have a very good idea whether these earlier cases proved profitable or the reverse and accordingly the premium and conditions which were applied to the earlier cases will serve as a starting point for his calculations.

Again, in the case which he is considering there may be certain factors which were not present in any of the earlier cases and he will endeavour to weigh up how these are likely to affect the situation. Some may appear likely to operate to his advantage—in which event they will almost certainly be emphasised by the Broker—whilst others may seem likely to be detrimental. To the man in the street it would probably be a matter of great difficulty to visualise more than a very few of the many different factors which might affect any given case, and it would be a matter of still greater difficulty to assess these in terms of money as does an Underwriting Agent when he quotes a premium. However, to an experienced Underwriting Agent, whose daily occupation is to weigh up probabilities in connection with the numerous insurances which are continuously being put before him by Brokers at Lloyd's, these matters become almost second nature, and it may indeed be said that some individuals have in course of time developed what has earlier been described as a kind of "underwriting instinct."

This does not mean that Underwriting Agents never make mistakes in their summing up of propositions for which no more or less established systems of rating and conditions have been evolved but nowadays so various are these different insurances, so many are the countries to which they relate and so divergent are the hazards with which they are concerned, that between them they make up what in practice generally proves to be a satisfactory average so that losses on some of these miscellaneous cases are usually counterbalanced by profits on others.

It is clear that in the ordinary course of events business will go to those Agents who are prepared to grant the most attractive rates and conditions and naturally different Agents will often reach very different conclusions as to what would appear to be suitable rates and conditions for any given case which they are offered, but it is at times somewhat surprising to find how very similar are the conclusions regarding a given case arrived at by different Agents who are known to employ very different methods in approaching their problems.

Of course, even in a free market such as exists at Lloyd's where all Underwriting Agents are in competition with each other and free to quote such rates and conditions as they choose, it not infrequently happens that what may be termed a "prevailing market rate" exists for a certain insurance or class of insurance. However, when this happens it is usually due to a gradually developed and unwritten general understanding and is seldom, if ever, the result of any definite agreement between different Underwriting Agents.

Apart from an Underwriting Agent's primary activities (viz., the selection of business and the examination of claims), there are of course many matters to which he has to attend. Not the least important of these are the investment and care of the moneys, in the shape of premiums and reserve funds, which he holds in trust on behalf of his Names, and also the keeping of his accounts in such a manner that from them can be ascertained the detailed information about his business which has to be supplied in conformity with certain very strict regulations laid down by the British Government and by the Committee of Lloyd's.

While the activities of Underwriting Agents are manifold, those of Lloyd's Brokers are generally far more diversified due to the fact that an Underwriting Agent deals only with Brokers, whereas a Broker has to deal not only with the Agents at Lloyd's but also with his Clients. A very important point in this connection which frequently is not realised by persons unacquainted with the structure of Lloyd's is that while a Lloyd's Broker is primarily an intermediary and essentially the servant of his Clients, he nevertheless, when transacting business at Lloyd's, relieves the Underwriting Agents and their Names (i.e., the Insurers) of a great amount of labour and expense which in the case of other types of Insurers falls on the shoulders of the actual Insurers themselves.

For example, since neither Underwriting Agents nor their Names are in direct touch with the public, it follows that practically the whole of what may be termed the Production or Acquisition Cost of insurances effected at Lloyd's falls not upon those Agents but upon the Lloyd's Brokers, on whom likewise falls the greater part of the cost of handling and looking after the business even when it has been secured.

Being thus largely or entirely unburdened with travelling expenses, telephone and cable charges, correspondence with Policyholders and Clients, collection of premiums from Correspondents, and similar costly and troublesome matters—including even the preparation of Policies*—it will be seen that Underwriting Agents at Lloyd's are able to conduct their business with much lower overhead costs than have to be borne by most Insurers. Although this arrangement is of undoubted ultimate advantage to Lloyd's and to the Insuring Public which reaps the benefit in the shape of lower premiums, it certainly throws a heavy burden on the Lloyd's Broker.

Having referred in the preceding paragraph to the preparation of policies, it may be mentioned in passing that up to the time of the 1914-18 War a Lloyd's Broker, having prepared a Policy, had to leave this for signature at the Boxes of the various Underwriting Agents whose initials appeared on his "Slip".† This system entailed a great waste of time and much unnecessary labour for both Brokers and Underwriting Agents and nowadays Lloyd's Brokers leave Policies which they have prepared, with the corresponding Slips, at a central Bureau, i.e., Lloyd's Policy Signing Office, where all Policies are examined and signed on behalf of the Groups concerned, each of which is supplied by the Bureau with such particulars of the Policies so signed as are required by each Group for the purpose of making up its accounts, etc.

As will be readily understood, many of the policies (numbering nearer two than one million in the course of a

* Except in the case of one or two types of Insurance (notably Automobile) all Lloyd's Policies are prepared by Brokers.
† See page 46.

year) which are issued at Lloyd's are in respect of insurances of a comparatively small and fairly routine nature to which more or less regularly recognised rates of premium and conditions are applied. The placing of these types of business is, of course, a fairly simple matter and does not call for any particular skill on the part of the Broker. However, it is unlikely that any Broker could make much of a livelihood merely out of the handling of these comparatively stereotyped smaller cases, and his success will largely depend on his ability to deal satisfactorily with larger insurances, the rates or conditions for which are not governed by any generally accepted custom. It is here that a Broker's skill, experience and initiative come into play, and he must continually be on the alert to learn how different Underwriting Agents are viewing different classes of business so as to know from what Agents he is likely to secure on behalf of his Clients the most favourable terms and conditions for any cases which he has to handle. This is not always an easy matter since in a community like Lloyd's, where the individual's freedom of action is so pronounced, it can happen at any time that an Underwriting Agent may change his methods or embark upon some new line of business.

On receiving an enquiry from a Client the Broker will collect such information and data regarding it as he believes will enable him to give a complete and lucid explanation of the case to those Underwriting Agents whom he thinks might suitably be approached in the matter. This obviously calls for specialised knowledge since, apart from the fact that the many insurances which Brokers are called upon to handle relate to all conceivable kinds of undertakings and risks in all parts of the World, it is obvious that no two cases of any importance are ever likely to be identical in all their features.

Although in his negotiations with different Underwriting

Agents the Broker will be acting as the Agent for his Clients, for whom he manifestly will seek to obtain the lowest premium and most favourable conditions, he must at the same time be careful to see that he obtains from his Clients all material facts relating to the case and that these are disclosed to the Underwriting Agents.*

When desirous of obtaining a quotation or arranging an insurance, a Broker will normally prepare a Memo, commonly called a "Slip," on which are set out brief particulars of the case with which he is dealing, and armed with this Slip he goes to the different Underwriting Agents whom he considers are most likely to be attracted by his proposal. They, if interested, may write on the Slip the terms and conditions which they require and should the Broker have a firm order they will put their initials on the Slip, setting against their initials the amounts or shares which they are willing to accept for their respective Groups. Thus, a Broker's Slip relating to a large case which he has completed may bear the initials of perhaps forty Groups which, in turn, represent in the aggregate perhaps a thousand or more separate Names. Having finally completed his Slip on terms which are acceptable to his Client, a Broker, pending preparation and signature of the actual policy, usually then sends his Cover Note or Charge Note to the Client.

Should the case with which the Broker has to deal be a large one, the completion of which would necessitate the participation of a number of different Groups, or if it is of a type which essentially calls for the consideration of an Underwriting Agent with specialised knowledge of that particular type of insurance, the Broker will in all probability

* It is an established principle of Insurance practice that omission (even if inadvertent) at the time of making an application for insurance, to disclose a material fact which is known to the prospective Assured (i.e. Policyholder) gives an Insurer (whether this be a Lloyd's Underwriter or an Insurance Company) the right to repudiate any claims which may subsequently arise on this insurance.

first approach one or more of those Agents who are looked upon as leaders in the market. These leaders are in constant demand and at each of their Boxes one often finds a queue of several Brokers waiting their turns to do business— occasionally, and especially in busy periods of the year, a Broker may thus have to spend perhaps an hour or even more in waiting to see a particular Agent. The delays to which a Broker is thus subjected are undoubtedly a hindrance and a serious waste of his time, but these are comparatively minor drawbacks in comparison to the outstanding advantages of a system which allows opportunities for frequent personal intercourse between individual Brokers (as the representatives of their Clients) and different Underwriting Agents (as the representatives of these Clients' Insurers or potential Insurers).

Under these circumstances it is obvious that a Broker may find it well worth his while to spend considerable time in waiting to see some particular Agent, knowing that when he does eventually see him he will be dealing with someone who, after a discussion lasting perhaps but a few minutes, will give him a definite "yea" or "nay" to any proposal and who can forthwith accept either the whole of the insurance under discussion or such a substantial proportion of it that the Broker, on the strength of the lead thus obtained, can be reasonably sure of completing the balance with other Agents. Depending on the nature and size of the case with which he has to deal a Broker may, of course, consider it desirable to get the independent views of a number of different Agents, since although one may not be prepared to interest himself, another might be willing to do so, subject possibly to certain modifications in the conditions or terms first proposed by the Broker.

It is often necessary for the Broker to exercise considerable judgment and discretion in deciding what particular Agents he is first going to approach for a lead. This is especially important if the case with which he has to deal is somewhat difficult to handle or if its completion would require the participation of a large section of the market, since if he, or for that matter any competing Broker, seeks to obtain the independent views of an unduly large number of different Agents before the final choice of a lead has been made, this may quite easily "spoil the market," so making it difficult or impossible to complete the insurance on as favourable terms as might otherwise have been secured.

Without in any way detracting from the credit which is due to the general run of Underwriting Agents at Lloyd's for the open mind which they display when invited to consider any novel insurance proposals or ideas, it is a fact—which most of these Agents would admit unreservedly—that very many highly successful innovations and developments in the field of Insurance are initially and in large measure due to the ingenuity of those Lloyd's Brokers who have profited by being brought up in the progressive atmosphere of Lloyd's where new ideas are far from being condemned merely because they are "new-fangled."

Anyway, irrespective of who were the actual authors, it is worthy of note that many forms of Insurance which but a few years ago were practically unknown and which at first were transacted only at Lloyd's and then only as isolated cases have been gradually developed and have proved so popular with the public that they can now be grouped into definite and important classes by themselves. Where this has happened it has undoubtedly been to the ultimate benefit of the public since, generally speaking, where business is transacted in large volumes better averages are secured and consequently more attractive rates and conditions can be obtained by the public than would be the case if only isolated transactions were being handled.

However, it is only fair to remark that the position at Lloyd's in regard to what may be described as miscellaneous Non-Marine transactions is nowadays very different from what it was in the closing years of the last century when practically no underwriting except in connection with Marine business was transacted. All credit is therefore due to those pioneers at Lloyd's who had the initiative and temerity to venture into entirely new and unknown fields by undertaking various Non-Marine insurances of which neither they nor anyone else had ever had any experience. They undoubtedly required, and showed, courage since they had absolutely nothing beyond an instinctive "underwriting sense" to guide them as to what rates of premium would prove profitable, while, moreover, the volume of Non-Marine business which can at first have come to them must have been so small that it could not possibly have been considered as constituting a satisfactory average.

That their outlook and views were essentially sound and that others have profited by their example is made amply evident by the really amazing way in which the seeds which they planted but some fifty years ago have since developed. It may truly be said that not only Lloyd's but Commerce and Industry as a whole owe a great deal to those pioneers whose enterprise assuredly was the commencement of Lloyd's as a market for innumerable types of Non-Marine Insurance, many of which at first were regarded elsewhere in the Insurance Market as being unorthodox in the extreme, but are now eagerly competed for by other Insurance Organisations as important and perfectly legitimate branches of their business.

CHAPTER VI

Can Holders of Lloyd's Policies Rely Upon Lloyd's Reputation for "Fair Dealing"?

THE final test of the value of the insurances which are granted (or sold) by any Insurance Organisation is exactly the same as the test which is applied by the purchasers of any other commodity, viz., whether or not the purchasers receive value for their money.

That Lloyd's comes through this test with flying colours is clearly demonstrated by the support which it has received from that vast body, the Insuring Public, whose ultimate judgment in a matter of this kind affords as sound a criterion as can be sought for. It is obvious that but for this support its growth would have long since been arrested—but far from this having happened it has for two centuries and more gone from strength to strength—while its rapid development since the beginning of the present century as a market for Non-Marine Insurance has been truly remarkable. The reasons for this are not hard to find.

Nowadays, far more than formerly, in all walks of life and in all matters, are our actions controlled and affected by endless laws and rules and regulations—and because of the complexities of modern civilisation we have to rely to a great extent on the written word. However, just because of these complexities we find, time and again, that the written word is difficult of interpretation or, if strictly interpreted, leads to a state of affairs which was not contemplated by parties who entered into an agreement. It is very largely because of the ability of its Members to adjust their methods to changing and unforeseen conditions and, when difficulties arise, to deal with these in a broad-minded manner, that Lloyd's occupies the position which it does.

Bearing in mind how vastly different are conditions to-day from those which obtained when Lloyd's first came into being in its early and primitive form, it is rather surprising that for so long it should have been able to serve the public so efficiently. Without doubt the explanation is partly to be found in the fact, already stressed, that at Lloyd's individualism is given every encouragement with the important proviso, however, that strong discouragement is given to any individual action which might detract from the well-deserved reputation for fair dealing which successive generations of its Members have built up.

At the time some 200 years ago when Lloyd's Coffee House was beginning to come into prominence as an Insurance centre and for long afterwards, the laws and customs governing Insurance matters were still in their infancy so that such business as was transacted at Lloyd's was perforce conducted very largely on the basis of general intention rather than legal obligation. The negotiating and granting of insurances was essentially a very personal affair in which one individual often did his business direct with another. Under these circumstances, when few, if any, laws existed for the protection of Policyholders, it was natural that those who desired to safeguard themselves by insurance sought out those "Underwriters" of olden times in whom they had real confidence and who could be relied upon to fulfil their engagements in the spirit rather than in the strict letter of the contracts into which they entered.

In such circumstances all individuals competing for business at Lloyd's were encouraged—if only from motives of self-

interest—to interpret their engagements in a broad-minded
fashion and from this there in turn developed at Lloyd's a
well-founded tradition for fair dealing. It is in this tradition
that generations of Underwriting Agents and practising
Members have been brought up.

Lloyd's unquestionably affords a very striking example of
an institution where conservatism and originality march
abreast and to the Committee at times falls the unenviable
task of holding the balance fairly between these two con-
flicting characteristics. However, the potent force in maintaining this balance is what perhaps can best be described
as the "Public Opinion of the Room" since there is no doubt
that the Room as a whole is ever fully alive to the *general*
harm which would result from the adoption, even on the
part of but one or two people connected with Lloyd's, of any
methods or practices which were not in keeping with the
great reputation which Lloyd's has for so long enjoyed.

Accordingly, while there is unquestionably considerable
competition between the different Groups of Names which
together comprise Lloyd's and at least as severe competition
between the different firms of Brokers which work at Lloyd's,
nevertheless they all have one interest in common, viz., that the
good name of Lloyds should be upheld. This is not a mere
matter of sentiment but is rather due to the realisation that the
happening of anything which tended to discredit Lloyd's in
the eyes of the public would, to a greater or less degree,
adversely affect the influx of business to Lloyd's—and no one
at Lloyd's could tell how far this might not in turn affect
him personally.*

Now obviously, the business or primary aim of each
Underwriting Agent is to write as large a volume as he can
of profitable insurances for the particular Group or Groups

* See page 65.

of Names for which he writes. It therefore follows, since Underwriting Agents for the supply of their business are entirely dependent on Lloyd's Brokers and since every Broker is free to deal with whatever Agents he chooses, that each Agent will seek to encourage Brokers to give him personally a "good show" of business—that is, to afford him as many opportunities as possible of considering and, if he so wishes, of writing shares in the insurances which these Brokers handle.

To encourage Brokers to give him a "good show" it is palpably necessary that an Underwriting Agent should make himself useful to Brokers. This consists of much more than just offering attractive rates, since the securing of an order and the issuing of a policy are but early—and by no means necessarily the most important—steps in the handling of any Insurance transaction. Rather it means that in his own interests he must be prepared consistently to adopt, not merely a fair, but indeed a definitely broad-minded attitude in regard to many matters with which he has to deal, since an Underwriting Agent who came to be looked on as being "trying to work with" would stand little chance of obtaining from Brokers the "good show" of business on which his success depends. Especially would this be so in the case of an Agent who gave the impression of being "difficult" over the settlement of claims since it is self-evident that a Broker, to preserve his own connections, must be absolutely sure that claims which he presents on behalf of his Clients will be dealt with in a reasonable manner.

The initial concerns of a person requiring insurance against some particular contingency are, firstly as to whether he can obtain it and secondly as to how much—or rather how little—he need pay for the protection he requires. As regards the first point, although it is a popular fallacy that any and every contingency can be insured against at Lloyd's, it is nevertheless beyond question that Lloyd's always has been and still maintains its position as the market for many types of Insurance which are regarded as quite unorthodox by many other Insurance Organisations, while as regards the second point it is equally certain that the rates of premium obtainable at Lloyd's for most recognised forms of Insurance (many of which first originated at Lloyd's) are highly competitive.

At the same time, it is equally obvious that the readiness of Underwriting Members of Lloyd's to engage in new and untried forms of insurance and to quote competitive rates and conditions would not alone account for the success which has been achieved and it is interesting to consider some of the other factors, really of greater importance, which have contributed to this success.

An Insurance Policy is, of course, nothing more than a contract or agreement entered into between two parties, viz., the Policyholder on the one hand and the Insurers on the other hand, and according to this agreement the Insurers undertake that in consideration of the Policyholder performing certain acts, notably paying them a premium, they will in turn perform certain other acts, notably pay losses in certain eventualities.

It is self-apparent that the amount of premium paid for an insurance (whether effected at Lloyd's or elsewhere) is usually comparatively trifling in relation to the amount which the Policyholder anticipates being able to recover should he sustain a loss such as is covered by his policy. Accordingly, while he assuredly will not wish to pay a higher premium than necessary, his ultimate and far more vital concern is to have the certainty that if and when claims arise which fall within the terms of his policy, these will be fairly dealt with by his Insurers. Unless he is satisfied that his Insurers not only have the ability (i.e., the necessary financial resources) to carry out their engagements but that they also have every intention of so doing, his policy can only be of questionable value.

The ability of Lloyd's Underwriters to meet their engagements is, of course, beyond question.* As regards their good faith, not only is this evidenced by the reputation which they have built up, but from what has been written it will be seen that, even if only from motives of self-interest, each Underwriting Agent at Lloyd's has every incentive to deal with claims in a reasonable and equitable and broad-minded manner which accords with the traditions of Lloyd's.

Having more than a little bearing on this point is the fact that one of the most important functions of a Lloyd's Broker is to assist his Clients in the presentation of any claims which they may have occasion to make and to obtain satisfactory settlement of these. Everyone will recognise that in certain respects the ultimate interests of an Insured (i.e., a Policyholder) and of his Insurers (whether these be Insurance Companies or Lloyd's Underwriters) are and must be directly opposed. An Insured wishes to pay no larger sum in premiums than is necessary and when he sustains a loss wishes to recover as much as he can from his Insurers. Conversely, the Insurers wish to secure as high rates of premium as they can and when settling claims do not want to pay out any larger sums than are reasonable.

Whilst one can assume that any reputable Insurers, whether Insurance Companies or Lloyd's Underwriters, are undoubtedly out to gain the goodwill of, and to give a fair deal to, their Policyholders, the fact remains that instances must at times occur where as between the Insurers and a Policyholder perfectly legitimate differences of opinion arise, e.g., in regard to the extent of the former's liability for a loss.

Now the average Policyholder is not an expert in Insurance

* See Chapter X.   E

matters and consequently is more or less handicapped should
he have to discuss any technical questions or difficulties with
his actual Insurers, who, of course, are experts.

In this respect the holder of a policy which has been
arranged by an efficient Broker unquestionably has certain
very definite advantages—and as has already been pointed out,
a Lloyd's Policy can only be arranged by a Lloyd's Broker.
Here, in any negotiations or difficulties with the Insurers'
expert representative, i.e., the Underwriting Agent, the
Policyholder is represented by another expert, the Lloyd's
Broker, who not only is acting as the agent of his Client (the
Policyholder) but whose personal interests are essentially
bound up with those of his Client.

A Broker's very existence depends upon his ability, through
his expert knowledge and experience, to acquire and retain the
goodwill of his Clients. Since obviously there is no more
certain way of discouraging business or of losing Clients than
failure to secure for them fair and proper settlement of claims
when these arise, it is patent that the Holder of a Lloyd's Policy
can count on expert and invaluable assistance from his Brokers
in connection with any claims which he may have occasion
to make.

Thus, apart from the very natural pride which Lloyd's takes
in maintaining its high traditions of the past, it will be seen
that a very real spirit of fair dealing must inevitably develop
and prevail in a community where business is conducted under
the unique conditions which exist at Lloyd's, where—through
Lloyd's Brokers—the Insuring Public can, and does, make its
voice heard to a very effective degree.

CHAPTER VII ·

Explaining How Some Firms at Lloyd's Act in the Dual Capacity of Brokers and Underwriting Agents

FOR the sake of simplicity in the preceding Chapters all references to an Underwriting Agent have been couched in such terms as would be employed were the Underwriting Agent an individual.* We must now endeavour to clarify certain matters regarding which a great deal of misconception undoubtedly exists in many quarters outside Lloyd's, viz., as to the position and activities of those firms, both Partnerships and Limited Liability Companies, which work at Lloyd's in the dual capacity of Brokers and of Underwriting Agents.

It has earlier been made plain that when, as at Lloyd's, there are no rules governing the terms and conditions on which insurances may be accepted, the selection of business calls for the exercise of individual judgment—and obviously can only be carried out by an individual. Also it is obvious that a person who proposes to seek election as an Underwriting Member of Lloyd's may often, and in most cases does, consider it desirable to appoint some other more expert and experienced party to act as his Underwriting Agent and in this capacity to deal on his behalf with the selection of business and the settlement of claims. Here, however, the prospective Member of Lloyd's is faced with a difficulty, since it is not by any means always an easy matter to find an individual who

* See footnote on page 29.

has proved underwriting ability and who is prepared to increase the number or size of the Groups for which he already acts as Underwriting Agent.*

It has already been pointed out that out of the 2,300 or so Underwriting Members at Lloyd's a considerable proportion consists of individuals, who, although duly elected as Underwriting Members, do not themselves actively work in person at Lloyd's—amongst these are to be found many prominent Merchants, Manufacturers, Industrialists, Bankers, etcetera, whose regular daily occupations are quite unconnected with Lloyd's. Of the remaining Underwriting Members of Lloyd's (i.e., those who are actively engaged at Lloyd's) only a comparatively small number spend their time in work which is directly connected with underwriting—the great majority are persons who are Partners or Directors or on the staffs of firms of Lloyd's Brokers, and primarily occupy themselves in the insurance broking business carried on by their firms. Such persons must obviously employ someone else to look after any underwriting business in which they as individuals wish to engage.

It must be remembered too that the public has not access to Lloyd's and that those members of the public who require insurance at Lloyd's can only obtain this through some firm of Brokers, with the result that the names of many Lloyd's Brokers are well known to the public which, however, seldom even hears of those individuals at Lloyd's who act as Underwriting Agents. Consequently when some person unconnected with Lloyd's contemplates seeking membership of Lloyd's he will normally ask for information and advice from some firm of Lloyd's Brokers whom he knows and holds in

---

* This generally results either from the terms of the Agent's agreements with his existing Names or from the fact that the Agent fears lest an increase in the number of his Names will prove detrimental to his earlier Names owing to the difficulty of securing a larger volume of business without deteriorating its quality.

good regard and in many cases he will seek to arrange with this firm that it will look after and manage the business in which he individually is proposing to engage as an Underwriting Member of Lloyd's. If the firm agrees to such an arrangement it becomes the official Underwriting Agent for that person, but it will obviously be necessary for the firm to employ some suitable and experienced individual who in "the Room" at Lloyd's will in person carry out the actual specialised operation of underwriting for that person. Thus in those cases where a Member of Lloyd's appoints a firm of Brokers as his Underwriting Agent the firm is really acting in a managerial, rather than in an underwriting, capacity and the actual underwriting is done by some individual who in effect can be considered as an Underwriting Sub-Agent appointed by the firm.*

As the practice grew for an Underwriting Agent to represent a Group consisting of a number of separate Names it became customary for the Agent, when presented with a policy for signature, to impress this with a rubber-stamp setting out the various Names comprised in the Group for which he had accepted a share, at the same time signing his name "as Agent" against the rubber-stamp impression. As mentioned in Chapter V, all Lloyd's policies are nowadays signed and sealed at Lloyd's Policy Signing Office where, however, the earlier practice of signing the policy by means of rubber stamp impressions of the different Groups subscribing it has now been discarded (except in cases where a policy is subscribed by either one or two Groups only.)

The present method, whilst undoubtedly quicker and more

* Apart from the case where a firm of *Brokers* acts as the official Underwriting Agent for some Group of Names there are certain other cases where the Underwriting Agent for a Group is not an individual but a firm. In these latter instances the firm generally consists of certain experienced Underwriting Members of Lloyd's who do not engage in broking but have formed a partnership for the specific purpose of carrying on the business of Underwriting Agents and Managers. However, seeing that such firms do not act as Brokers we are not really concerned with them in the present Chapter.

practical, less clearly brings home to a layman the centuries-old characteristic of individualism which is such an interesting factor in the general set-up of Lloyd's. Accordingly, for the purpose of the following example which will help the Reader to understand how Groups may come into existence, we will use the earlier system of signing—but for obvious reasons the names or titles of the individuals or firms mentioned in this Chapter are purely imaginary.

The principal figure in our example is a gentleman whom we shall call Mr. Britain, who, as a young man, achieved the position of Deputy or chief assistant to a certain established and successful Non-Marine Agent, Mr. Wales, then under-writing for a fairly large Group of Names. At that time it happened that a Mr. Niton and a Mr. Vistock (who, as Partners in a firm of Lloyd's Brokers trading as Cornwall, Devon and Co., Ltd., were Subscribers to Lloyd's) decided to become Underwriting Members. Being admirers of Mr. Wales's methods, they would have liked to arrange with him to underwrite for them, but he was not disposed to accept any further Names.* So, having noticed the ability displayed by his Deputy, Mr. Britain, they turned their minds to him.

They then learnt of certain other Members of Lloyd's who up till then had confined their underwriting activities to Marine business, but had become desirous of engaging also in Non-Marine business. These other Members (some of whom were themselves Brokers at Lloyd's) on being approached by Mr. Niton and Mr. Vistock fell in with the suggestion that between them they should form an entirely new Group of Names, for which the Non-Marine Under-writing Agents should be Messrs. Cornwall, Devon & Co., Ltd., provided that they could arrange for Mr. Britain to do the actual underwriting. In due course this was arranged,

* See footnote on page 58.

J

Form approved by Lloyd's Underwriters' Fire and Non-Marine Association.

LLOYD'S POLICY.

(Subscribed only by Underwriting Members of Lloyd's who have complied in all respects with the requirements of the Assurance Companies Act of 1909 as to security and otherwise.)

Any person not an Underwriting Member of Lloyd's subscribing this Policy, or any person uttering the same if, so subscribed, will be liable to be proceeded against under Lloyd's Acts.

Whereas BAKER AND SMITH LIMITED

of

(hereinafter called "the Assured"),   have   paid £25. 0. 0d. in full Premium or Consideration to Us, who have hereunto subscribed our Names to Insure against Loss as follows, viz.:—

£ 25,000.

Printed at Lloyd's, London, England. 9-4-37.

This Policy to indemnify the Assured for any sums which under the terms of their Contract dated 27th January 1937 with the Downshire County Hospital the Assured shall become liable to pay as the result of the happening during the currency hereof of any of the events described in Clause Number 14 of the said Contract.

during the period commencing with the **Twentyfirst** of **February, 1937** and ending with the   **Twentieth**   of **February, 1938** , both days inclusive.

If the Assured shall make any claim knowing the same to be false or fraudulent, as regards amount or otherwise, this Policy shall become void, and all claim thereunder shall be forfeited.

Now know We, that We the Underwriters do hereby bind Ourselves, each for his own part, and not one for Another, our Heirs, Executors, and Administrators, to pay or make good to the Assured or to the Assured's Executors, Administrators, and Assigns, all such Loss or Damage as aforesaid as may happen to the subject matter of this Insurance, or any part thereof during the continuance of this Policy ; not exceeding the Sum of TWENTY FIVE THOUSAND POUNDS STERLING,

such payment to be made within Seven Days after such Loss is proved and that in proportion to the several Sums by each of Us subscribed against our respective Names not exceeding the several Sums aforesaid.

In Witness whereof We, Underwriting Members of Lloyd's, have subscribed our Names and Sums of Money by Us insured.

Dated in London, the **Sixteenth** Day of **February,**   One Thousand Nine Hundred and **Thirty-seven**

SEAL of LLOYD'S POLICY SIGNING OFFICE.

(A)

Name		Share
H. O. Nixon	(d)	2/31sts
T. A. Vinnert	(c)	2/31ers
B. I. Cexer	(g)	2/31sts
C. Amborne	(d)	1/31st
S. U. Thurland		1/31st
H. E. Brides		1/31st
F. I. Feshir		1/31st
R. Oxburgh		1/31st
I. N. Verness		1/31st
P. Adstow	(d)	1/31st
A. N. Trim		1/31st
R. O. Scoamen		2/31sts
B. R. Idport	(f)	1/31st
S. Nowdon	(b)	2/31sts
S. T. Albans	(a)	1/31st
C. H. Ester	(c)	1/31st
L. I. Merick		1/31st
W. A. Terford	(h)	1/31st
W. Exford		2/31sts
U. T. Toxeter	(h)	2/31sts
W. Alsall		1/31st
S. Tirling		1/31st
C. R. Omary		1/31st
T. A. Unoa	(e)	1/31st

CORNWALL DEVON & CO., LTD.

Per *GBritain*

£2000

(B)

Name		Share
S. T. Ockton	(j)	1/6th
D. O. Hill		1/12th
S. A. Lodge		1/12th
A. C. Criagton	(l)	1/6th
C. Onsett	(j)	1/12th
B. O. Manor		1/12th
Q. Richmond		1/12th
H. A. Broadwg		1/12th
G. A. Tchead	(j)	1/6th

DURHAM BROS, & CO., LTD., AGENTS.

Per *GBritain*

£750

(C)

Per *GBritain*

Name		Share
G. BRITAIN		2/40ths
B. L. ANDFORD	(f)	1/40th
S. KENSINGTON		1/40th
C. R. EDSTON	(d)	1/40th
B. O. S. CASTLE	(d)	1/40th
N. H. GATE		1/40th
M. A. BLETHORPE	(o)	1/40th
A. RUNDEL	(n)	1/40th
B. O. WESPARK		1/40th
H. HEATH		1/40th
S. H. ERBORNE	(f)	1/40th
W. A. REHAM	(f)	1/40th
S. A. LISBURY		1/40th
E. A. LING		1/40th
B. R. ENTWOOD		1/40th
W. A. DEBRIDGE	(r)	1/40th
H. A. VERFORD	(l)	1/40th
C. O. VENTRY		1/40th
W. O. ODGREEN		1/40th
E. FINCHLEY		1/40th
C. A. M. BERWELL		1/40th
E. N. FIELD		1/40th
C. O. LINDALE		1/40th
H. I. WYCOMBE	(m)	1/40th
O. S. TERLEY		1/40th
T. R. OWBRIDGE	(t)	1/40th
P. E. TERSFIELD	(t)	1/40th
W. E. ALDSTONE		1/40th
S. W. ISCOT		1/40th
C. HESTERFIELD	(q)	1/40th
A. L. FRETON	(q)	1/40th
C. LAPHAM		1/40th
S. H. ADWELL		1/40th
M. A. IDSTONE	(n)	1/40th
A. M. BLESIDE		1/40th
S. Y. DENHAM	(p)	1/40th
E. L. LESMERE	(s)	1/40th
M. I. L. DENHALL	(k)	1/40th
B. O. ROUGH		1/40th

£3000

(NOTE.—The small letters in brackets, which would not appear on an actual Policy, show on Pages 62 and 63 with which firms of Lloyd's Brokers different Names are associated.)

Mr. Britain thus ceasing to be the Deputy of Mr. Wales and becoming instead a fully fledged Underwriting Sub-Agent employed by Cornwall, Devon & Co., Ltd.

It was not long before Mr. Britain's capacity for under-writing was fully proved and widely recognised, with the result that in the course of years numerous further Names or their Underwriting Agents sought that he should also conduct underwriting on their behalf. By no means could all of these be accommodated and for some considerable period after the formation of the original Group for which Cornwall, Devon & Co., Ltd., were acting as Underwriting Agents such additional Names as were selected were accommodated by enlarging this Group.

Later it was arranged that Mr. Britain—who, incidentally, by then had himself become a Member of Lloyd's—while continuing to act as an Underwriting Sub-Agent employed by Cornwall, Devon & Co., Ltd., to write for the Group for which they were the Underwriting Agents, should at the same time be free

      (*a*) to act as Underwriting Sub-Agent for certain *other* Underwriting Agents,

and also (*b*) to write for certain Names who desired to appoint him *directly* as their Underwriting Agent.

These changes naturally necessitated the formation at different times of separate further Groups—with the result that Mr. Britain is now writing for seven different Groups comprising between them well over 120 separate Names, in relation to some of whom he is acting as the actual Under-writing Agent, while in relation to others he is acting as Underwriting Sub-Agent.

It will help to make the position clear if we examine in detail three out of these seven Groups. On the accompanying

Plate is a reproduction of the standard "skeleton" printed Policy Form in general use at Lloyd's for Non-Marine insurances. On the face of the Policy are set out details of a hypothetical insurance for £25,000 of which shares aggregating £10,000 have been accepted by Mr. Britain for his seven Groups. In our illustration we show only the first of the reverse or inner sheets of the Policy and it will be seen that this sheet has been "signed" by three of Mr. Britain's Groups. His four other Groups and also the Groups of other Agents who participate in the Insurance must be imagined as having "signed" in like manner for their respective shares on the remaining sheets of the Policy.

It will be observed that although Mr. Britain's own signature appears against each Group, there appears in addition, in the case of each of the Groups A and B, the title of a firm of Lloyd's Brokers, these firms being the respective Underwriting Agents for all the Names in the Groups in question. In the case of Group C, however, each of the Names in the Group has individually and directly appointed Mr. Britain as the official Underwriting Agent.

In all three of these Groups are a certain number of Names who are not actively and personally engaged in work at Lloyd's, but the majority are so engaged. Thus, amongst the Names appearing in Group A for which the Underwriting Agents are Cornwall, Devon & Co., Ltd., are to be found a few individuals who are themselves Underwriting Agents (or Deputies to Underwriting Agents) for certain other Groups transacting Marine business, and a much larger number of other individuals who are or have been active Partners or Directors of, or otherwise directly associated with, the following firms of Lloyd's Brokers,* viz.:—

* The letters in brackets are explained in the footnote on the Plate.

1 with Bedford & Herts. (a)
1 „ Carn Arvon & Co., Ltd. (b)
1 „ Cheshire Flint & Co., Ltd. (c)
4 „ Cornwall, Devon & Co., Ltd. (d)
1 „ S. O. Merset & Co. (e)
1 „ D. Orset & Co., Ltd. (f)
1 „ Rutland Oxford & Co., Ltd. (g)
2 „ S. Tafford & Co. (h)

Likewise, in Group B, for which the official Underwriting Agents are Durham Bros. & Co., Ltd., we find Names who are active Directors or Partners respectively of the following firms of Lloyd's Brokers, viz.:—

1 with L. Ancashire Ltd. (i)
3 „ Durham Bros. & Co., Ltd. (j)

Coming now to Group C, we find that the Names appearing in this include, amongst others, persons who are or were active Partners or Directors of, or otherwise directly associated with, the following firms of Lloyd's Brokers, viz.:—

1 with C. Ambridge & Co., Ltd. (k)
1 „ W. Arwick & Co. (l)
1 „ Buckingham Bros. Ltd. (m)
3 „ Cornwall Devon & Co., Ltd. (d)
2 „ Kent Sussex & Co., Ltd. (n)
1 „ Lincoln & Rutland Ltd. (o)
1 „ W. Morland & Co. (p)
2 „ Notts Derby & Co., Ltd. (q)
3 „ D. Orset & Co., Ltd. (f)
1 „ Pembroke & Co., Ltd. (r)
1 „ S. H. Rops Ltd. (s)
3 „ Wilt Shire Hants & Co., Ltd. (t)

From the foregoing it will be seen that amongst the Names comprising Group A for which the Underwriting Agents are *one* firm of Lloyd's Brokers (Cornwall, Devon & Co., Ltd.), are persons who are actively engaged in the businesses

respectively carried on by *eight* entirely separate firms of
Lloyd's Brokers*—whilst amongst the 72 Names (comprising
these three different Groups) for whom Mr. Britain is underwriting are to be found persons who are actively engaged
in the businesses respectively carried on by no fewer than
twenty entirely separate firms of Lloyd's Brokers.

At first sight it may seem rather difficult to reconcile this
state of affairs with the fact that as Lloyd's Brokers every
one of these twenty different firms is, to a greater or less
degree, in active competition with the others.

Actually, however, there is nothing at all contradictory in
the position since no single one of these Names in his capacity
as an Underwriting Member takes any active or personal part
in, or has any control over, the actual operation of the underwriting business which, on his behalf, is carried on by his
duly appointed Underwriting Agent or Underwriting Sub-
Agent. The Agent has the widest powers to conduct this
business along whatever lines he thinks fit without any kind
of interference from his Names—it may indeed be said that
during the existence of an Underwriting Agreement between
an Agent and a Name the latter puts himself and all his
worldly possessions into the hands of and at the mercy of
this Agent.

Correspondingly, the Underwriting Agent or Underwriting
Sub-Agent is in no way concerned with any other business
which is carried on by the Name either as an Insurance Broker
at Lloyd's or in any other capacity.

If an individual has been elected as an Underwriting Member
and at the same time is, for example, a Partner in a firm of
Lloyd's Brokers, then the Agreement which he enters into
appointing some named party (whether a firm or an individual)

---

* Some of these, other than Cornwall, Devon & Co., Ltd., are themselves Underwriting Agents for certain Names.

as his Underwriting Agent is signed by him in a purely personal and individual capacity and this Agreement has nothing whatever to do with the firm in which he is a Partner.

The fact that amongst the Names comprising some Group or Groups which are underwritten for by a single Underwriting Agent or Underwriting Sub-Agent are to be found a number of persons connected with various firms of competing Lloyd's Brokers somewhat strikingly illustrates how, in spite of the existence of a very strong element of internal competition between different firms at Lloyd's, a large number of the Principals of these competing firms have very definitely one interest in common, viz., to maintain the high reputation of Lloyd's. Thus, while individual competition and personal freedom of action always have been and are very potent factors in the development and continued virility of Lloyd's, the widespread overlapping of the personal interests of so many individuals is of the utmost value in promoting a corporate outlook and in discouraging any individual action which might reflect on the good name of Lloyd's as a whole.

CHAPTER VIII

Opposition to Lloyd's

A VERY progressive institution like Lloyd's whose Members are untrammelled by hide-bound conventions and where personal initiative receives every encouragement is bound to be subjected to a certain amount of criticism and opposition, particularly from those who for some reason or another do not favour the introduction of new methods and new ideas—whilst further it is obviously in the very nature of things that any successful commercial organisation such as Lloyd's must expect competition. Thus it is only natural that at times various competitors, or concerns which harbour some real or fancied grievances against Lloyd's, will seek means whereby they can hinder or restrict the activities of Lloyd's or dissuade members of the public from effecting insurance at Lloyd's.

Most of the arguments which are advanced against Lloyd's take the form of very sweeping generalisations founded upon quite inaccurate and misconceived ideas of what Lloyd's really is and how it operates. It is to be hoped that from the explanations so far given in this Outline the Reader will already have obtained a sufficiently clear idea of Lloyd's to enable him to judge for himself whether or not any criticisms which he may hear directed against Lloyd's are justified. At the same time, it seems just as well to refer to one or two misleading assertions which, especially outside this Country, are time and again made by people who evidently

have, or appear to have, very little knowledge of Lloyd's and
its ways.

*   *   *   *

First and foremost of these comes the allegation that the
degree of financial security behind a Lloyd's Policy is of but
problematical and doubtful value. During the past few years
such assertions have been heard much less frequently than
formerly, but now and again they are still made in uninformed
quarters.

The question of the financial security behind every Lloyd's
policy is more fully discussed in Chapter X, but in the meantime it can be taken for granted that any person who sought
to impugn the financial strength of Lloyd's would be dis-
playing such abysmal ignorance that it would effectively
discredit the value of his views on any other matters concerning Lloyd's.

*   *   *   *

Another argument which is sometimes advanced against
Lloyd's is that if in relation to a Lloyd's Policy a dispute
arose which could only be settled in a Court of Law, since
each of the Names (of which there might be some hundreds)
on a Lloyd's policy is a separate entity, it might be necessary
for the Policyholder to bring a separate Law Suit against
each of all these different Names.

Whilst in theory such a possibility exists, there is not the
slightest likelihood that anything of this kind could or would
ever happen in practice. Although many millions of Lloyd's
policies have been issued, so far as is known no such happening
is on record.

From the point of view of the Names concerned, the bringing of a separate Law Suit on identical grounds against each Name would manifestly be an altogether undesirable and futile proceeding which inevitably would operate to the detriment of the Names themselves and from which they could secure no possible benefit. The verdict given in any Law Suit brought against one of the Names would merely be repeated in any separate Law Suits brought individually against the remaining Names and at the same time each Name would have to bear the whole cost of defending the action which was brought against him as an individual.

Accordingly, in the comparatively rare instances where a dispute in relation to a Lloyd's Policy gives rise to a Law Suit it is the invariable custom for all the Names concerned to appoint one of their number to defend what may be described as a "test case," the costs of which are then borne by these different Names in proportion to their respective interests in the Policy and the verdict given in this test case is then treated as applying to all the Names in question.

*   *   *   *

Sometimes too one hears statements to the effect that on the retirement or death of a Lloyd's Underwriter difficulties or delays will or may have to be anticipated in the settlement of claims on policies which had been underwritten by him. However, such statements are utterly without foundation.

As mentioned earlier, when any individual is elected as an Underwriting Member he has to comply with certain regulations laid down by the British Government and the Committee of Lloyd's, and as more fully explained in Chapter X, these conditions are such as to ensure that on the retirement or death of a Lloyd's Underwriter all contracts previously entered into by him or by an Underwriting Agent on his behalf are duly carried out in exactly the same way as if he had not retired or died.

*   *   *   *

Again, when from time to time some of those Insurance Organisations which set out to work on more mechanically scientific, and consequently more costly, systems than are in vogue at Lloyd's find themselves in competition with Lloyd's for business, they are often inclined to accuse Lloyd's Underwriters of unfair behaviour in the matter of fixing rates of premium. They contend that an Underwriting Agent at Lloyd's, who has made no contribution towards compiling the very extensive records and statistics which form the basis of many of the rates charged by these Organisations, is unfairly profiting by their labours when he bases his rate of premium for some particular case on the rate which is or would be charged for that case by one or other of these Organisations.

It would never be denied that such happenings do occur, but the occurrence is probably much less common than might be imagined from the frequency with which some competitors allege that Lloyd's indulges in unbridled rate cutting. Moreover, it can safely be said that the rates for the vast bulk of the business handled at Lloyd's are based on the personal judgment and experience of individual Agents rather than on the rates charged by external competitors.

Manifestly if Lloyd's Underwriters were merely copyists who never originated anything themselves but simply took advantage of their lower working costs to underbid competitors who had more scientific and consequently more expensive organisations, *and* if this were the whole story, more than a little sympathy might be felt for these competitors.

Actually, of course, the position is very different since it could be—and in some quarters is—contended that many competing Insurance Organisations themselves have unfairly profited, and continue to profit, from the initiative and originality displayed by Lloyd's Underwriters in venturing into and developing new and untried forms of Insurance.

The memories of the public are short-lived, but a noteworthy fact which must be borne in mind when considering the respective activities of Lloyd's and other Insurance Organisations is that until certain Lloyd's Underwriters first ventured outside the realms of Marine Insurance during the latter part of the Nineteenth Century, practically the only type of Non-Marine Insurance (apart from Life Assurance) which the public could obtain was insurance of actual tangible property against loss or damage by Fire. Insurance against Burglary or Theft or against such contingencies as Earthquake or Hurricane or Riots, let alone insurance against "All Risks," was unheard of, whilst in Insurance Circles outside Lloyd's* it would have been thought utter madness to suggest that it might be reasonable or practicable to insure a Manufacturer against any Consequential Loss or Loss of Profits which he might sustain were the operation of his factory interrupted by a fire or other accident.

All the foregoing, and countless other types of Non-Marine Insurance which have come into being since Lloyd's Underwriters first entered the field of Non-Marine Insurance in the latter part of last century, either originated at Lloyd's or for their initial development depended on the co-operation of some Lloyd's Underwriters, but the latter have seldom been long allowed to retain the full fruits of their initiative. It is easily within the memory of many persons now living that various well-established and highly reputable Insurance Companies were simply aghast and prophesied disaster when

* And also by not a few Members of Lloyd's.

certain Lloyd's Underwriters embarked on some of these then unorthodox and untried types of business—and yet as soon as these had stood the test of time at Lloyd's and proved their worth they were gladly taken up by these self-same Insurance Companies who, without any scruples, nowadays compete with Lloyd's for them.

Even from this alone it will be seen how manifestly the public profits by Lloyd's' activities and how completely unwarranted can be any kind of assertions that Insurance Companies would be better off and more efficient but for Lloyd's, or vice versa.

*   *   *   *

It is noticeable that in some Newspapers and Insurance Periodicals published abroad very considerable prominence is invariably given to any instance in which any Lloyd's Underwriters are involved in a Law Suit, and yet one seldom if ever reads of any instance where any well-known or reputable Insurance Company has repudiated or disputed a claim under a Non-Marine Policy.

That one but seldom reads of any Insurance Company being involved in a legal action concerning a Non-Marine Policy can without doubt be largely accounted for by the fact that the Non-Marine policies issued by Insurance Companies in England and certain other countries almost invariably contain a condition stipulating that any dispute or difference of opinion is to be settled by arbitration, which, of course, avoids the publicity entailed by an action in the Law Courts. Be this as it may, the fact remains that some of these journals unquestionably take every possible opportunity to create and foster the impression that, as compared with other Insurance Organisations, Lloyd's Underwriters are essentially litigious and difficult to deal with.

The hostility of certain of these periodicals to Lloyd's is further evidenced by some of the articles, usually anonymous, which at times appear in their pages and which are nothing less than definite attacks on Lloyd's. For the greater part these articles are so obviously and completely biased and so full of flagrant inaccuracies that Lloyd's can well afford to ignore them—and one is only left wondering how it can come about that these periodicals find it worth while to employ news-space in such a futile manner.

* * * *

In recent years there has been a definite tendency amongst Legislatures of different Countries and States to introduce laws designed to ensure that any Insurance Organisations operating in those Countries or States conduct their business on a financially sound basis. Manifestly some such legislation is very desirable for the protection of members of the public, many of whom have undoubtedly suffered from the activities of the numerous mushroom and fly-by-night Insurance Concerns which are to be found in many places where legislation of this kind does not exist. Further, it is quite certain that such legislation, if suitably framed, would not be objected to by any reputable and well-conducted Insurance Organisations.

However, it is the particular manner in which this legislation is framed which so frequently gives opponents of Lloyd's an opening for the furtherance of their own ends.

This comes about from the fact that when considering how best to ensure that proper security is available for the business carried on in a given Country by any Insurance Concern, ninety-nine out of a hundred individuals, when approaching the subject, will unquestionably—and not unreasonably—do so in the light of their knowledge of the financial structure of important Insurance Organisations with which they are well acquainted. Further, it can be taken for granted that probably every one of these organisations is constituted as a Company (either Joint Stock or Mutual) with Limited Liability.

Consequently, there is every likelihood that those drafting the proposed legislation will devise laws which are appropriate to, and only to, concerns which are so constituted—whereas, as pointed out earlier and as the Reader will certainly realise for himself on studying Chapter X, Lloyd's, London, bears no resemblance to a Company with Limited Liability but is a unique institution having a financial structure which, although absolutely beyond question, is without its counterpart anywhere in the World.

This affords a golden opportunity to the opponents of Lloyd's—since in most cases they are not slow to realise that its unique structure and the stringent ordinances which are imposed on its Members by the British Government render it impracticable and indeed impossible for Lloyd's to comply in the letter with certain financial regulations which can very reasonably and suitably be imposed on concerns constituted as Companies.*

These hostile elements naturally do not seek to educate the public as to the true position. On the contrary, knowing full well that the suggested laws, if passed as drafted, will seriously hinder the public from taking advantage of the insurance facilities offered by Lloyd's, they institute a campaign acclaiming the proposed legislation—which on its face is well meaning, and certainly is intended to protect the public—so long as it is made applicable to *all* Insurance Organisations.

Some of the arguments which they advance in support of their campaign are eminently plausible, and may well seem fair and reasonable to the man in the street who knows little or

* Why this is so will be more fully appreciated after perusal of Chapter X.

nothing of what Lloyd's really is and who does not know or realise that

1. All Lloyd's Underwriters have to conform to certain laws and stringent regulations which the British Government imposed in 1909 for the especial purpose of ensuring that adequate security exists for all holders of Lloyd's Non-Marine Policies throughout the World.

2. Since the passing of these laws there has been no single instance where, as a result of the failure of a Lloyd's Underwriter, any Holder of a Lloyd's Policy has not recovered the full amount legally due in respect of any *bona fide* claim made by him under a Lloyd's Policy.

Fortunately, however, there is clear evidence that the Governments and increasingly large sections of the public in many Countries and States are coming more and more to realise that Lloyd's Policies afford security which is second to none, and that although legislation may be necessary to protect the public against financially unsound Insurance *Companies*, such legislation must be so framed that the public can still benefit from the operations of Lloyd's Underwriters, whose methods of working and initiative prove of such marked assistance in meeting the continually changing requirements of Commerce and Industry by providing all manner of insurances on reasonable terms.

CHAPTER IX

Miscellaneous

IN this Chapter it is proposed to refer to various different matters regarding which considerable misapprehension often exists or information in regard to which is not infrequently sought for by people unconnected with Lloyd's.

*   *   *   *

Grave misconceptions regarding Lloyd's have undoubtedly been fostered in some quarters by the fact that in various Countries outside Britain there are sundry Shipping or Insurance concerns which have incorporated the name "Lloyd" or "Lloyds" in their titles.

It certainly is testimony to the high repute in which Lloyd's has always been held that other concerns entirely unconnected with it have thought it to their advantage to describe themselves in this manner—but it is a compliment which at times proves inconvenient and disadvantageous not only to Lloyd's itself but also to the public.

Some of these Insurance Concerns, in whose title the word "Lloyd's" is prominent, and also their methods are fairly well known in the cities or localities in which they work. It is therefore not unnatural that in such places there are many people whose sole ideas of Lloyd's, London, are based on their knowledge of the practices and standing of these purely local organisations which, for their own ends, have assumed the name of "Lloyds."

It cannot be too strongly stressed that neither the methods

75

of working nor the financial structures of any of these self-styled "Lloyd's" have any resemblance to those of the real Lloyd's whose name they have seen fit to copy.

* * * *

In many quarters outside Lloyd's misuse is very often made of the term "Lloyd's Agent," and a common mistake is to describe as a Lloyd's Agent any firm which makes a business of obtaining Lloyd's Policies for those of its Clients who desire to secure insurance protection at Lloyd's.

At a great many seaports and inland centres in various parts of the World are to be found certain individuals or firms whom the Committee of Lloyd's, in consultation with Marine Insurance Companies, has duly appointed as official "Lloyd's Agents", but such individuals in their capacity as Lloyd's Agents have no kind of authority to accept insurances for Lloyd's and their duties are in general very different from those of the appointed Agents of an ordinary Insurance Company. It should always be remembered that Lloyd's, that is to say the Corporation of Lloyd's, does not itself grant insurances and that when an insurance is effected at Lloyd's this is granted not by Lloyd's Underwriters as a body but merely by certain individual Lloyd's Underwriters.

The general intention of an Insurance Company when appointing an Agent is that the latter should be active in securing business for the Company which he represents, but the primary object of the Committee of Lloyd's when selecting and appointing an individual to act as a "Lloyd's Agent" in some given locality is to ensure that, if required, a properly qualified person will be available to act promptly on behalf of any interested Lloyd's Underwriters or Marine Insurance Companies in cases of losses arising in that locality under any Marine Insurances which have been effected at Lloyd's or with these Companies. It also, of course, happens on occasions that some interested Lloyd's Underwriters may instruct a Lloyd's Agent to deal with a claim under a Non-Marine or Aviation Policy. A Lloyd's Agent will also act in sundry other matters —for example he will be expected to send in reports of any local happenings which might appear to be of interest to the Committee of Lloyd's—but for the greater part his activities relate to matters requiring attention in connection with claims under Marine policies.

In very few cases does a Lloyd's Agent receive any kind of regular salary or retaining fee,* and such services as he carries out on behalf of any Lloyd's Underwriters in connection with claims are paid for by the particular Lloyd's Underwriters concerned in the claims. On a vacancy occurring there is usually considerable competition for the post of Lloyd's Agent—not so much because of any direct financial benefit expected therefrom but because of the undoubted "kudos" which an individual obtains through holding the appointment.

It is seldom that a Lloyd's Agent is a person whose business activities are solely confined to Insurance matters. For the greater part Lloyd's Agents are selected from the ranks of well-established and reputable firms carrying on some kind of business (such as that of Exporters or Shipping Agents) which brings them into contact with various matters connected with marine insurance procedure and practice.

Such firms, when so appointed, seldom consider the appointment as anything except a side-line—albeit one of which they may be proud—to their main business and similarly amongst these firms are to be found some who at the same time also run an Insurance Brokerage business as a side-line to their main business. Naturally, when so acting as an

* This might, however, be given in very special circumstances—for example where a Lloyd's Agent appointed to some important port has to devote a lot of time to collecting and reporting movements of shipping, etc.

Insurance Broker, it is more than likely that such a Firm, in view of its relations with Lloyd's, will make use of Lloyd's as a market for such orders as it receives but, of course, it will not be able to negotiate these orders direct with any Lloyd's Underwriters but only through some firm of Lloyd's Brokers in London.

It will thus be seen that although a firm which has been duly appointed as a Lloyd's Agent may at the same time occupy itself as an Insurance Broker obtaining Lloyd's Policies for its Clients, this side of the firm's business has nothing whatever to do with the Lloyd's Agency which the firm holds. Similarly, the fact that an Insurance Broker makes a practice of supplying his Clients with Lloyd's policies certainly does not constitute him a Lloyd's Agent.

Whilst on the subject of Lloyd's Agents it is necessary to deal with a point which occasionally and quite understandably gives rise to misapprehension. At times it happens that a firm of Lloyd's Brokers is able to make certain arrangements on behalf of some particular firm of Insurance Brokers which is established abroad whereby this latter firm, although having no official connection with Lloyd's, is empowered to accept insurances of a particular type on behalf of certain specified Lloyd's Underwriters. In these special circumstances the firm to which these facilities have been granted may, in a manner of speaking, be considered the Agent for certain specified purposes of the particular Lloyd's Underwriters concerned, but this most certainly does not constitute it a Lloyd's Agent and were the firm so to describe itself it would immediately be pulled up by the Committee of Lloyd's.

* * * *

The foregoing references to officially appointed Lloyd's Agents whose primary function is to act for interested Lloyd's

Underwriters and Marine Insurance Companies in connection with losses which arise in their localities under Marine Insurance policies, calls to mind another body which, although not actually a part of Lloyd's, is very closely connected therewith. This is the Salvage Association, formed a number of years ago by Lloyd's Underwriters and Marine Insurance Companies jointly to deal with salvage questions arising in connection with claims under Marine Insurance policies.

To quote from "A History of Lloyd's" the Salvage Association, since its inauguration, has been " . . . a centre of friendly action for the common good. In other departments of insurance business, competition and rivalry naturally exist; but in the work of salving property, minimising loss, repairing damage, and remunerating meritorious service, the Committee and staff are only concerned in promoting the profit and welfare of all the interests committed to their charge."

* * * *

Another organisation which is very closely connected with Lloyd's, although not—as many suppose—an actual part thereof, is Lloyd's Register of Shipping. This is a Society controlled by a Committee consisting of Representatives of Lloyd's,* Marine Insurance Companies, Shipowners, Shipbuilders and others who are vitally affected by matters relating to the proper construction and upkeep of all types of vessels. The Society annually publishes the world-famed Lloyd's Register of Shipping, ordinarily referred to merely as Lloyd's Register, which contains *inter alia* the names, classes and detailed information concerning the vessels classed by Lloyd's Register and the late Underwriters' Registry for Iron Vessels; particulars, as far as possible

---

* On the Committee of Lloyd's Register, Lloyd's is represented by the Chairman of Lloyd's for the time being and eight other elected Members.

of all sea-going vessels in the World, and of all iron and steel vessels trading on the North American Lakes, of 100 tons and upwards. The Society further publishes Lloyd's Register of Yachts and Lloyd's Register of American Yachts, and also a number of volumes giving rules and scientific data relating to all manner of subjects which are of interest to Naval Architects, Shipbuilders and others. Surveyors of the Society are stationed throughout the world for the purpose of supervising both the construction of vessels (including the testing of all materials used therein) intended to be classed as "A1"* and also their subsequent maintenance and repair.

*   *   *   *

Every now and then paragraphs are to be found in different newspapers giving particulars—which are seldom very complete or accurate—about some freak insurance which has been effected at Lloyd's, and which it is apparently thought will make interesting reading. Also not infrequently statements appear in the Press to the effect that such and such a premium is being quoted by Lloyd's to insure against the happening of some particular contingency regarding which speculation is rife in the minds of the public. For example, one may read that a Policy has been arranged at such and such a premium to insure against some given tax or customs duty being altered within a stated period or to insure against some political party securing a majority at an impending election. The publication of statements of this nature is very misleading and gives rise to considerable misunderstanding in various directions.

Perhaps the most unsatisfactory feature of this publicity is that it causes some people who have little knowledge of insurance matters to get the impression that business as

* See page 89.

No. in Book. Official No. Code Letters	Steamer's Name. Material, Rig, &c. Late Name if any. No. of Decks, &c. Special Surveys	Register Tonnage. Gross. Under deck. Net.	Particulars of Class' fication. Character. Port of Survey.	Date when and where Equipment now surveyed Letter	Built. When Ship. By Whom. Where.	Owners.	Regist'd Dimensions, &c. Deck Erections, &c. Length. Breadth. Depth.	Port of Registry. Flag.	Engines.	Moulded depth.
80821 302 J8BO	Quadrifoglio (exRocco-40, exGlenTilt, exHartside) Welldeck D.F. E.S.D. GyO. Mchy.Aft Elc.welded	661 666 388	✠ ... 7,26 ✠		1888 2mo D.Baxter & Co. Sunderland	Carmine Vitiello	190·0 28·7 13·2 184·9 Q62'B45'F28'	Torre del Greco rx Italian	0.2Cy.25"&48"−30' R.&W.Hawthorn,Nwc. WB	13·10
80822 246740 KYVR	Quaker Hill Welldeck D.F. E.S.D. GyO. Fitted for oil fuel Cruiser Stern Mchy.Aft Carrying Petroleum in bulk Elc.welded Longitudinal framing	10172 — 6184			1944 Alabama D.D.&S.B.Co. Mobile,Ala.	United States WarShipping Administration	504·0 68·2 39·2 P108'B36'F63'	Mobile,Ala. Utd.States	Steam turbine connected to elec. motor & sc. shaft General Electric Co. Lynn, Mass.	
80823 C89D	Quansa (exPortugal) TwinSc D.F. E.S.D. ssShl.No.3−6,34 ssShl.No.2−43 2Dk,3rd dk in Nos.1,2&3holds Cruiser Stern Ref.Mchy.	6636 4131 3944	Lis 100A1 withfreeboard 10,45 M88,43 NBmade14fitted29	2†	1929 Blohm & Voss Hamburg Lloyd's AP	Cia. Nacional de Navegacao	418·2 52·6 28·6 P&B271'F86' Cell DB347'1001t FP782t Tanks at sides of tunnel 19'166t	Lisbon Portuguese rx 9 BHCsm	T.6Cy.22½",35½",a66½"− 47½" 218D (s) rD 986M N471' BHB,Bef,aa848,ms14694 Blohm&Voss,Hamburg	31 0 6 5 24 11
80824 193541 MDZT	Quaysider ssGun.2ndNo.3−3,39 ssShl.No.1−44 Welldeck 1Dk(Stl) Mchy.Aft Cargo battens not fitted	616 432 301	Hul 100A1 LMC 11,45 BS11,45	✠ LMC7 44	1918 11mo J.P.Renoldson&Sns. SouthShields. Lloyd's AP	F.G.Browne	175·3 28·2 11·0 Q89'B9'F22' rx 5 BHCsm. Cell DB112'1140t FP7444A PT81t	Newcastle British	T.3Cy.16½",26"&41"−27" (s) 180tb 95RP J.P.Renoldson&Sns.S.8hl	13 3 4 2 12 8
80825 243844 KPHD	Quebec D.F. E.S.D. GyO. Fitted for oil fuel Cruiser Stern Mchy.Aft Longitudinal framing Elc.welded Carrying Petroleum in bulk	10420 — 6298	1Dk		1943 5mo KaiserCo. Inc. Swanland, Or. Lloyd's AP	United States WarShipping Administration	504·0 68·2 39·2 P108'B36'F63'	Portland, Or. Utd.States	Steam turbine connected to elec. motor & sc. shaft General Electric Co. Lynn, Mass.	
80826 133460 VGQB	[no name] TwinSc ssMct.No.3−5,41 1Dk(Stl)2nd dk in holds Carrying Petroleum in bulk	7018 2481 4143	Qbo ✠ 100A1 withfreeboard LMC 4,45 M85,41 BS84,45	⌘ P10,43 n3,45	1928 5mo Davie,S.B. &Rpg.Co.Ld. Lauzon,P.Q. Lloyd's AP	Canada Steamship Lines,Ld.	350·1 70·0 18·8 rx 8 BHCsm Cell DB278' 519t FPT1126A PT87t	Montreal British	T9Cy.31⅜"e(3⅜)46"−36"(s) 190tb 100D 790M N 6SB,18c/geS830,ms12656rD Richardson,Westgarth& Co.Ld.Hpl	21 0 5 2 16 11

			For Service between Fitted for oil fuel 5,		Montreal 28	& Saguenay F.P. above 1	50° F.							
80827 148518 GKWS	**Queda** ssCal.No.3–6,37 ssCal.No.1–41 2Dks(Stl)&Shelter dk(Stl)	7766 7184 4760	✠100A1 withfreeboard 4,46 Examined4,46 ✠LMC MB3,45 BS12,45	Mdb	s†	CL 6,45	1925 1mo Lloyd's A4CP	W.Gray& Co.Ld. W Hartlepool	BritishIndiaStm. Nav.Co.Ld. CellDB429' 1703t DTa81'976t	487·0|60·7|29·9 F45' FK FPT195t APT27t	London British 8BHptCem (Coll toSh dk 7 „ 2nd „)	Q.4Cy.28½",41",58½"&85" –54" (s) 225lb 933MN 5SB,18cf,GS361,HS14253 Cen.Mar.E.Wks.Ld.WHpl	32 " 8 FD 35 " 1½ 27 " 9½	
80828 130979 VDPR	**Quedoc** (exKamaria,exMariska) Mchy.Aft 1Dk	3072 2623 1874					1890	GlobeIron WorksCo. Cleveland,O	PatersonSteam- ships,Ld.	346·4|40·2|22·0 H—F36' len23 WB	Fort William, Ont. British	T.3Cy.24½",38"&61"–42" GlobeIrnWksCoCleveland		
80829 164093 GZCL	**Queen Adelaide** Oil Eng. D.F. E.S.D. ssGls.No.1–41 1Dk&Shelter dk CruiserStern Tonnage opening closed '41(W.E.)	4933 4558 2993	✠100A1 withfreeboard 1,46 Examined 1,46 ✠LMC CS12,41 DBS4,45 4,39	Avn	a† 2	CL 3,45	1936 9mo Lloyd's A4CP	Barclay, Curle&Co.Ld. Glasgow	QueenLine,Ld. (T.Dunlop&Sons, Mgrs.) CellDB360'1393t MT32' 1234t	418·2|55·2|25·5 431·5(O.L.) F40' FK FPT119t APT95t	Glasgow British 7BHptCem (Coll to Sh dk 6 „ 2nd „)	Oil Engines 2S.C.SA 3Cy.20½"–81½" 387MN 2DB120lb Barclay,Curle&Co.Ld.Gla.	37 " 7 11 " 1½ 26 " 8½	
			Carrying veg etable			oil in deep tank								
80830 20612	**Queen City** Mchy.Aft 1Dk	3785 — 2367					1896	Cleveland S.B.Co. Cleveland	UnitedStates WarShipping Administration	401·4|48·0|28·7 WB	Duluth, Minn. Utd.States	T.3Cy.23",38"&63"–40" ClevelandS.B.Co.Clevelnd.		
80831 166290 GBSS	**Queen Elizabeth** QuadSc D.F. E.S.D. GyC. Radar Sub.Sig. 5Dks,6th&7thdks clear of mchy.space, CruiserStern 8th dk fwd.of mchy.space (Topsides–special quality steel)	85000	✠100A1 withfreeboard 11,45 Examined 11,45 BS6,45 ✠LMC2,40 Ref.Mchy. (See separate section) Fitted for oil fuel 2,40	Sou	††	CL Pf4,45 Pa5,44 Sf5,44 Sa5,44 F.P. above 1	1940 2mo Lloyd's A4CP 50°F	J'hnBrown &Co.Ld. Clydebank	CunardWhiteStar, Ld. CellDB820'6658t D	987·4 |118·6| 68·4 1031·0(O.L.) B&F875' UpperB567' FK Tsf124'1586t FPT2	Liverpool British 15BHptCem ptAsp 91t APT281t	16 steam turbines SR geared to 4 sc. shafts 35210MN 12WTB475lb(Spt450lb) HS246000 FD JohnBrown&Co.Ld. Clydebank	74 " 5 s33 " 0½ 41 " 6½	BT till 6,46
80832 133048 GGNR	**Queen Empress** PadSp 2Dks	411 291 164					1912	Murdoch & Murray,Ld. PortGlasgow	CaledonianSteam PacketCo.Ld.	210·0|25·6| 8·4	Glasgow British	C.D.2Cy.27½"&54"–54" Rankin&Blackmore,Grk.		
80833 164282 GBTT	**Queen Mary** QuadSc D.F. E.S.D GyC. Radar CruiserStern 5Dks,6th&7th dks Sub.Sig. clear of mchy.space, 8th dk forward of mchy.space (Topsides–special quality steel)	81235 56152 34120	✠100A1 withfreeboard 1,46 BS5,45 ✠LMC5,36 Fitted for oil fuel5,36	Sou	††	CL 10,42 F.P. above 1	1936 5mo Lloyd's A4CP 50° F.	J'hnBrown &Co.Ld. Clydebank	CunardWhiteStar, Ld. CellDB885'8585t	975·2 |118·6| 68·5 B715'F93'Upper Bridge540' FK DT/38'695t FPT3	Liverpool British 15BHAsp 10t APT364t	16 steam turbines SR geared to 4 sc. shafts 446lb (s) 33653MN 24WTB(Spt425lb) HS234000 FD 3DB250lb(Spt) JohnBrown&Co.Ld.	74 " 7 s33 " 5½ 41 " 4½	BT till 5,46
80834 161974	**Queen Mary II** TrpSc (exQueenMary–35) 2Dks&Shelter dk	870 572 336					1933	W.Denny &Bros.Ld. Dumbarton	CaledonianSteam PacketCo.Ld.	252·5|35·1|10·1	Glasgow British	3 steam turbines W.Denny&Bros.Ld.Dmb.		BT till 1,47

QUA-QUE

A PAGE FROM "LLOYD'S REGISTER" SHOWING ENTRY FOR "QUEEN ELIZABETH"

conducted at Lloyd's consists for the greater part in the granting of very out-of-the-way and speculative insurances which to the layman may well appear to be little more than wagers or bets. In point of fact the number of insurances of this description which are effected at Lloyd's is an absolutely insignificant proportion of the insurance business which is conducted there and of which the vast bulk relates to matters which certainly would not be looked upon as "news" likely to be of interest to the ordinary general reader of a newspaper. Further, the few insurances having a "news value" which are effected are usually for paltry amounts the whole of which is accepted by perhaps but one or two Underwriting Agents who possibly happen to have certain small commitments in other directions which would be conveniently counter-balanced by the acceptance of the insurances in question.

Thus, just because one reads in some newspaper that some particular rate of premium has been paid at Lloyd's to insure that some particular event does or does not take place, it must not be assumed that this premium reflects the concensus of opinion of Lloyd's Underwriters as a whole. Far from this being the case it is highly probable that the vast bulk of the many different Underwriting Agents at Lloyd's were never even approached in regard to the insurance in question—and that had they been approached they would not have been disposed even to discuss it.

*   *   *   *

Some of the irresponsible and sweeping statements which are made at times regarding the position of Lloyd's Under-writers *vis-à-vis* Insurance Companies would almost lead one to believe firstly that as between Lloyd's on the one hand and Insurance Companies on the other there exists a spirit of implacable bitterness and secondly that of these two great communities one was deserving of all commendation and the other of all condemnation. As to which community was supposed to be deserving of whole-hearted commendation or condemnation will depend on the personal interests of the individual making these statements, but in any case any such statements, especially when—as unfortunately is sometimes the case—they are made by persons who should know better, are greatly to be deplored, and in the long run can only do harm to insurance interests generally.

It must be remembered that just as at Lloyd's there is often keen internal competition for business between different Groups of Underwriters, so equally Insurance Companies often compete very keenly between themselves for business—but it is noticeable that such competition arouses nothing like the comment which is called forth on divers occasions when certain Groups at Lloyd's are found to be in competition with certain Insurance Companies. On these occasions to suggest, as some people seem inclined to, that Lloyd's Underwriters are banded together in a war against all other Insurance Organisations or that all Insurance Companies are banded together in a war against Lloyd's is utterly misleading.

It would, of course, be idle to suppose that there was at all times entire and complete harmony between all Lloyd's Underwriters and all Insurance Companies since obviously there are and must be dissimilarities in certain of the problems with which each of these communities respectively has to deal. Such dissimilarities are probably much more frequent in the field of Non-Marine business than where Marine Insurance is concerned seeing that the latter is essentially of an international character and that the fundamental practices and theories relating to it are the same the whole world over, being founded almost entirely on those which were gradually developed at Lloyd's. Moreover, in Marine underwriting, whether conducted by an Insurance Company or by a Lloyd's

Underwriter, it is clearly impracticable to employ any kind of mechanical or cut-and-dried methods when selecting business or fixing premiums since these are essentially matters for individual experience and judgment. Accordingly although the "Underwriter" for a Marine Insurance Company may be competing with a Marine Underwriting Agent at Lloyd's, each will approach business from very much the same angle.

However, to a much less degree is this the case in the field of Non-Marine Insurance. Because of the manner in which it is constituted and the consequent necessity for delegating authority to numerous employees, an Insurance Company must perforce lay down fairly rigid rules governing the selection and rating of Non-Marine business—whereas at Lloyd's a Non-Marine Underwriting Agent works in much the same way as his brother Marine Agent who, while paying due regard to any statistics or data which are available, relies primarily on his own personal experience and judgment.

Thus, in the underwriting of Non-Marine Insurance there are two quite separate systems or schools of thought. One is typified by the Insurance Companies, believing in the application of more or less mechanical methods and the other is typified by Lloyd's, conducting business along much more elastic lines. Only a very biased partisan would ever maintain that either method was wholly beyond criticism or that either was definitely superior to the other in every direction—but whatever may be the defects in the Lloyd's system the encouragement and opportunities which it affords for individual enterprise and originality are of undoubted benefit to the public.

That these characteristics of Lloyd's are fully recognised and appreciated even by competitors and that these self-same competitors—despite anything some of their over-zealous officials or representatives may at times say to the contrary—have every faith in the good name and standing of Lloyd's is clearly shown by the fact that innumerable British, European, American and other Insurance Companies, including many of the largest and best-known in the World, themselves make very extensive use of Lloyd's as a reinsurance market.

Inventions of a mechanical nature can be patented but, irritating or disappointing as it may be to pioneers in the field of Insurance, it is just as well for progress that there is no "Copyright of Ideas." As mentioned earlier, many forms of Non-Marine Insurance which were originated by certain Lloyd's Underwriters were before long adopted by others at Lloyd's, and have since been taken up by a great many Insurance Companies who, by developing and advertising these, have undoubtedly done much to educate the public as to the value of these forms of Insurance. Whilst it can certainly be said that these Insurance Companies, in thus copying many ideas which originated at Lloyd's, have undoubtedly profited by the initiative and courage displayed by those Lloyd's Underwriters who first ventured into these earlier untried branches of Insurance, it is equally true that the activities of these Insurance Companies have helped to make the public "insurance minded," and have stimulated public demand which, in turn, is of definite benefit to Lloyd's.

*　　*　　*　　*

Although already referred to in preceding Chapters it here seems relevant again to refer to an important fact, which is not altogether unrelated to the preceding paragraphs, and which many members of the public either do not know or else fail to appreciate, viz., that while Lloyd's Underwriters may only accept business which is offered to them through a duly authorised Lloyd's Broker, there are no corresponding restrictions of this kind upon Lloyd's Brokers. That is to say, a Lloyd's Broker who receives an enquiry or order from a Client regarding some insurance is perfectly free (unless otherwise instructed by his Client) to offer or arrange this wherever he chooses, either wholly with Lloyd's, or wholly with one or more Insurance Companies, or partly with Lloyd's and partly with Insurance Companies. Thus a Lloyd's Broker has at his disposal the whole of the Insurance Market in London made up of both Lloyd's and Insurance Companies, and he can utilise whatever particular section or sections of this market he considers or finds to be the most suitable for each particular case with which he has to deal on behalf of his Clients. Many firms of Lloyd's Brokers undoubtedly make extensive use of Insurance Companies and the business, both Marine and Non-Marine, which Lloyd's Brokers annually arrange with Insurance Companies (as distinct from Lloyd's Underwriters) must in the aggregate amount to an immense figure.

Bearing in mind that a Lloyd's Broker will, in his own interests, seek to handle his Clients' insurances in the most efficient manner possible, and that he is free to deal with such Lloyd's Underwriters or such Insurance Companies as he chooses, the large amount of business which Lloyd's Brokers arrange with both of these two communities plainly shows firstly that neither the Company system nor the Lloyd's system of underwriting is invariably the most advantageous to the public, and secondly that in many directions and to no small degree Insurance Companies and Lloyd's Brokers are mutually useful to each other.

*   *   *   *

Another point which is not always clearly appreciated by members of the public is that although a Lloyd's Broker normally acts as the servant or agent of his Clients (and not as the agent of any of the Groups of Lloyd's Underwriters with whom he does business)* he makes no charge to his Clients

* See page 34.

for his expert services either when arranging an insurance or when subsequently looking after it, except that a small fee is sometimes payable for the collection of certain types of claims.

When any member of the public purchases securities on the Stock Exchange he has to pay a commission to the Stock Broker who negotiates the transaction, or, again, a member of the public who requires legal advice and consults a Lawyer has to pay a fee to this Lawyer—but the Clients of an experienced Lloyd's Broker can count on receiving gratuitously expert assistance and advice in regard to all manner of insurance problems.

What has just been written brings us to consider the somewhat anomalous fashion in which the Lloyd's Broker is paid for the services he renders. Although he is not the agent of the Lloyd's Underwriters with whom he arranges insurances nevertheless it is from them that he receives his remuneration in the form of a commission on the premiums which he collects from his Clients and pays to these Lloyd's Underwriters.

In certain respects it might be said that from the Broker's point of view this is not a particularly attractive arrangement since every reduction in premium which he manages to secure for his Clients has the effect of adversely affecting his income, but nevertheless the system has stood the test of time and in practice works satisfactorily. Anyone having intimate knowledge and experience of the service which a conscientious and expert Lloyd's Broker affords both to his Clients and to the Lloyd's Underwriters with whom he transacts business will undoubtedly agree that the Broker very fully earns any remuneration which comes his way.

*   *   *   *

A question which is often asked is as to the manner in which an Underwriting Agent or Underwriting Sub-Agent at

Lloyd's is remunerated by the Names for which he writes. This is purely a matter of agreement between a Name and his Agent, but usually the remuneration takes the form of an annual fixed fee which is payable by the Name irrespective of the result of each year's business, together with a commission on the profits, if any, which accrue to the Name on the business which has been carried out on his behalf by the Agent in the course of the year. Naturally there are considerable divergences in the forms of Underwriting Agreement entered into between different Agents and their respective Names, and also in the terms of remuneration received by different Agents. In good years some of these undoubtedly receive substantial rewards for their labours, but at the same time it must be remembered that an Agent carries great responsibility, that special qualifications are required to be a successful Agent, and that all years are not good years. If he succeeds in making money for his Names they will certainly not grudge him his commission.

*   *   *   *

As already explained it is the various individual Members of Lloyd's who in the aggregate comprise the Corporation of Lloyd's, and it is these individual Members of Lloyd's who elect from amongst themselves the Committee of Lloyd's for the purpose of looking after the interests of the Members as a whole.

However, within the general structure of Lloyd's there are certain further Associations, each with its own Committee, these Associations having been formed for the purpose of dealing with matters which more especially concern certain sections of the general community at Lloyd's.

The oldest of these is Lloyd's Underwriters' Association, comprised of all Groups of Lloyd's Underwriters, the Agents for which engage in Marine Insurance business. That there is

o

nothing in the title of this Association to indicate that the activities of its Members are primarily or entirely of a Marine Insurance nature is accounted for by the fact that when this Association was first formed Lloyd's had not seriously entered the field of Non-Marine Insurance, and for all practical purposes transacted nothing but Marine business, so that the term "Lloyd's Underwriter" in itself had a Marine Insurance significance.

There are other Associations of Lloyd's Underwriters, viz., Lloyd's Underwriters' Fire and Non-Marine Association (ordinarily spoken of either as the Non-Marine Association or merely as the N.M.A.), and Lloyd's Motor Underwriters' Association and Lloyd's Aviation Underwriters' Association. The titles of these indicate the respective spheres of activity of their Members.

Further, there is Lloyd's Insurance Brokers' Association (ordinarily referred to merely as the Brokers' Association) comprised of firms of Lloyd's Brokers engaged in any description of Marine, Non-Marine or Aviation Insurance.

The main functions of the Committee of each of these Associations are to promote the interests of the Members of the Association it represents, and to deal with matters which more especially affect these Members, but since there is so much interlocking and overlapping of the interests of all parties working at Lloyd's, it can be said that the work undertaken by these Committees is in no way of a parochial nature but is of direct benefit to Lloyd's as a whole. Their respective Committees provide a convenient channel for official intercourse and exchange of views between the different sections of the general community working at Lloyd's whilst further, the Committees of Lloyd's Underwriters' Association and of the Brokers' Association are in frequent and close touch with the Committee of the Institute of London Underwriters, which latter body comprises all the important Marine Insurance Companies operating in London and which obviously have many interests in common with Lloyd's.

*   *   *   *

As is known to all Readers of this Outline, the qualifying term "A1" has, for generations past, been popularly employed throughout the World as a means of describing something as being of the best. However, it is not realised by all how this expression came to acquire its meaning or how it came to be used so universally in this sense.

This symbol had its origin at Lloyd's and dates from the early days of Lloyd's Register of Shipping.* Then, as now, the Compilers of the Register grouped different vessels into different classes according to their respective merits, these classes being distinguished by different symbols, of which in earlier times "A1" was the symbol reserved for the very best class of vessel.

By reason of the high reputation enjoyed by Lloyd's and its fame in all countries, this expression "A1" came, in course of time, to be adopted by the World at large as a qualifying term which would signify beyond all possible doubt that some particular thing or matter or arrangement is of the highest merit and comparable with the highest standards as adopted by Lloyd's, itself an Institution of the highest standing.

* See pages 15 and 79.

CHAPTER X

The Financial Security Behind Every Lloyd's Policy

WE now come to the second and very important question which, as mentioned in Chapter I, it is the purpose of this Outline to answer and explain, namely, What financial security is afforded to the Holder of a Lloyd's Policy?

The Reader who does not wish to investigate the actual details for himself but is prepared to be guided by the views of others whose judgment should be as critical as it is possible to obtain, will undoubtedly feel that this question is fully answered by the following facts:

1. *The Bank of England and every British Bank accepts without question a Lloyd's Policy for any amount for which it is offered.*

> That such Banking Institutions with their world-famed and well-deserved reputation for caution should thus avail themselves of the facilities offered by Lloyd's is in itself ample testimony to the standing of Lloyd's. .

2. *British, European, American and other Insurance Companies, including most of those whose names are household words throughout the World, themselves make extensive use of Lloyd's as a market in which to re-insure what are often large portions of the direct liabilities which they have undertaken through issuing their own policies to the General Public.*

> Since an Insurance Company which issues a policy is solely responsible to the Policyholder for the due fulfilment of its obligations thereunder and could not claim to be exonerated

from any of these because of the failure of some institution with which it had re-insured a portion of its liabilities, and since the great Insurance Companies are pre-eminently well qualified to judge the standing of Lloyd's, it is manifestly unimaginable that many of these would thus re-insure at Lloyd's had they any doubts as to the financial security of Lloyd's Underwriters.

Conclusive as is the foregoing, some Readers may wish to have some actual details of the safeguards which are provided for the Holders of Lloyd's Policies, and we will now set out to give a general explanation of the very strict requirements which the British Government, in conjunction with the Committee of Lloyd's, imposes on all Members of Lloyd's and which ensure that there is unquestionable financial security behind every Lloyd's Policy.

In this connection it seems desirable to revert to one or two important features which characterised Lloyd's in its early Coffee House days when it was nothing or little more than a meeting place for individuals who not only worked "each for his own part, and not one for another," but who, moreover, were not required to conform to any laws or regulations designed to ensure that they were capable of meeting their financial obligations.

In those days, when business was of a very personal nature, it was naturally important to every individual Lloyd's Under-writer that he should have a personal reputation for stability, since lacking this reputation such business as was being offered at Lloyd's would naturally trend towards others who frequented Lloyd's and who were held in higher repute—but to the general community then working at Lloyd's the failure of an individual can have been little more than an unfortunate incident since at that epoch the frequenters of Lloyd's traded on their personal reputations rather than on the reputation of Lloyd's as a whole.

However, as Lloyd's grew and became increasingly well-known as an important Insurance Centre, so more and more did it become evident that any happening which reflected unfavourably on the credit of even a single member of Lloyd's would adversely affect the interests of Lloyd's as a community.

Although as time went on there inevitably developed a definite corporate spirit at Lloyd's, it cannot be denied that up to the early years of the present century the Holder of a Lloyd's Policy, particularly a Non-Marine Policy, had little, if any, direct evidence of the financial standing of the particular Lloyd's Underwriters with or by whom he was insured. Admittedly since 1870 every Member of Lloyd's had been required to put up certain deposits on his election to Lloyd's, but these deposits were not of a very substantial nature and, further, they were specifically held as security for Marine insurances undertaken by that Member. It is true that the Holder of a Lloyd's Policy could have great confidence in this by reason of the reputation which over 200 years or more Lloyd's had built up for fair dealing and security, but the fact remains that he had very largely to accept a Lloyd's Policy merely "on trust."

Although after 1870 when a system of Deposits was first introduced, various further safeguards were initiated from time to time, it was not until 1908 that any real progress was made in the direction of adopting measures which would absolutely ensure that there was adequate and definite security behind all Lloyd's Policies.

In that year the Committee of Lloyd's was able to make one of the most important announcements in the whole history of Lloyd's, namely that every Lloyd's Underwriter had voluntarily agreed to allow his Underwriting Accounts to be investigated annually and reported upon by independent

Auditors specially approved by and working under the directions of the Committee.

This annual investigation, which came to be known as "the Audit," was—and to a much greater extent nowadays is—far more than an Audit in the commonly accepted sense of that term. It is more fully dealt with later in this Chapter, and for the moment it will suffice to say that the Audit is *a system of proved efficiency designed to prevent an Insurer from getting into such a position that the eventual interests of his Policyholders may be imperilled.*

Faced as they were with an organisation like Lloyd's, for which no parallel existed anywhere in the World, those who in 1908 set out to formulate the original terms of "the Audit" were indeed presented with a formidable task, since it was their aim to devise a system

(*a*) which would not unduly hamper the invaluable and almost inviolable right of the individual Lloyd's Underwriter or his Underwriting Agent to conduct his underwriting business in his own particular way,

(*b*) which would make certain that adequate and definite security was always available for all Holders of Lloyd's Policies,

(*c*) which would make due allowance for the very important factor that *all Lloyd's Underwriters (unlike the Shareholders or Members of a Joint Stock or Mutual Insurance Company) are individually responsible to the whole extent of their entire personal fortunes for the fulfilment of their underwriting commitments.*

As the Reader will realise the last factor is a very valuable safeguard to the Holders of Lloyd's Policies, since not only must it represent an enormous, although indefinite, "cash reserve," but it is the strongest possible evidence of "good faith."

Seeing that from the earliest days of Lloyd's, before any specific financial safeguards were ever thought of, business had been conducted and developed on practically no other foundation than the all important one of "good faith," it was obviously essential for those originally devising "the Audit" so to frame it that this element of good faith would continue to play the vital rôle which it had always played in the affairs of Lloyd's, even although effective financial safeguards were provided in addition.

Time has shown that the very novel provisions of the original "Audit" of 1908 were most brilliantly conceived and worked out, and that they achieved to a truly remarkable degree the different objects which those formulating it had in view. The provisions as first applied have since been gradually further developed as experience has shown that they could be tightened up and improved upon, but it is singular testimony to those who conceived and drafted the terms of the 1908 Audit that none but minor weaknesses have ever come to light in the very original theories which they first propounded.

In the following year came yet another event which ultimately proved to be of the utmost importance to Lloyd's and to all Holders of Lloyd's Policies. This was the enactment by the British Government of The Assurance Companies Act of 1909, which, as may be gathered from its title, was originally devised and primarily intended to regulate the operations of Insurance *Companies*. The main purpose of the Act in question was to impose legislation which would make certain, so far as was reasonably practicable, that adequate financial security existed for all Holders of Non-Marine Insurance Policies issued by Insurance Organisations working in Britain.

However it was realised by the British Government (which at all times has shown itself to be fully alive to the valuable services which Lloyd's renders to the public) that regulations which were suitable for Insurance Companies were quite inappropriate to and could not be conformed to by Lloyd's Underwriters, so there was added to the Act a separate section* laying down certain regulations which had to be complied with by all Lloyd's Underwriters who were undertaking Non-Marine insurances.

No more impressive evidence of the high repute of Lloyd's could be afforded than the fact that after fully investigating the procedure which Lloyd's had already *voluntarily* adopted in order to ensure that there would always be adequate security for all its Policyholders the British Government approved this procedure "lock, stock and barrel", and embodied it in the 1909 Act as a statutory procedure thereafter to be complied with by Lloyd's Underwriters in respect of Non-Marine insurance business. Whilst under the 1909 Act the audit became a statutory requirement in respect of Non-Marine business only, under the domestic regulations of the Committee of Lloyd's the audit continued to apply to *all* classes of business conducted by Lloyd's Underwriters and the form of Auditors' Certificate prescribed by the Board of Trade in connection with Non-Marine business was adopted by the Committee in respect of all other business.†

The provisions of the Assurance Companies Act, 1909 have been amended by the Assurance Companies Act, 1946, and under the new Act statutory requirements have been introduced in respect of Marine insurance business. In the case of Lloyd's Underwriters these requirements follow the

* Schedule 8.
† The Act allowed for an alternative procedure but the Committee, being of the opinion that this alternative was far less stringent and effective, never sanctioned it for use by any Members of Lloyd's.

safeguards adopted by the Committee of Lloyd's since 1908 and the audit test to which Marine business conducted by Lloyd's Underwriters has been subjected for close on 40 years has been accepted by Parliament for the purposes of the new Act.

Much more far reaching and beneficial results than could originally have been visualised arose out of the voluntary adoption by Lloyd's Underwriters of the principle of "the Audit," and the subsequent embodiment of this in the 1909 Act as a statutory regulation, since one effect was to give the Committee of Lloyd's very much wider powers of control than it had ever previously had over the finances of the Members of Lloyd's.

The wide powers which were thus vested in the Committee have enabled successive Committees (for each one of which the present and future stability of Lloyd's has naturally always been a matter of greatest importance) gradually but surely to impose more and more stringent rules on Members with the result that there now exist infinitely greater safeguards for the protection of Holders of Lloyd's Policies, both Marine and Non-Marine, than would have been achieved merely by compliance with the minimum requirements and provisions of the Assurance Companies Act.

Many millions of separate insurances must have been effected at Lloyd's since 1909, and claims paid out to Holders of Lloyd's Policies during the same period must amount to an immense figure—certainly in excess of even such a vast sum as £800,000,000—but it is noteworthy that although since the passing of the 1909 Act heavy losses have been sustained at different times by members of the public through the failure of various Insurance Companies, and although during the same period a few individuals who were Members of Lloyd's have become insolvent there has not been a single instance where the failure of a Lloyd's Underwriter has caused a pennyworth of loss to any Holder of a Lloyd's Policy making a legitimate and bona-fide claim thereunder.

Let us now review some of the formalities and stipulations which have to be complied with by an individual before he can become an Underwriting Member of Lloyd's.

Presumably before considering applying for membership the candidate would take steps to make sure that some particular Underwriting Agent* would be prepared to act for him were he duly elected. Having assured himself on this point he would have to find an existing Underwriting Member who would be willing to sponsor his application for membership, and the candidate, together with his sponsor, would be required to attend before a Sub-Committee who would enquire fully into the status, both financial and otherwise, of the candidate, and decide whether in their view he was in every way fitted to undertake the responsibilities attaching to membership of Lloyd's. As regards the financial status of the candidate, this would have to be vouched for by means of a Certificate signed by his Bankers, Solicitors or Accountants. If, after the enquiry conducted by the Sub-Committee, the Committee of Lloyd's are satisfied as to the suitability of the candidate, his nomination as a Member would have to be supported not only by his sponsor but also by 5 other Members of Lloyd's.

Deposits.

As part security for his underwriting business a Member is required to lodge a substantial Deposit with the Committee of Lloyd's in the form of readily negotiable gilt-edged securities. These securities stand in the name of the

* See page 57.

Corporation of Lloyd's, but so long as everything goes satisfactorily the dividends on the securities are paid direct to the Member.

The amount of the Deposit varies according to the type and volume of business which the Member proposes, through his Underwriting Agent, to transact. At different times the Committee has laid down scales, each more drastic than the last, stipulating the varying amounts of Deposit required from a Member according to the respective volumes of Marine and Non-Marine business separately which he desires to be able to transact.

Persons who are not very intimately acquainted with Lloyd's sometimes seem to assume that the Deposit which every Member has to make with the Corporation in connection with his underwriting business can be considered as the equivalent to the Share Capital of an Insurance Company. Actually, of course, it is nothing of the kind and *it is much more in the nature of an unencumbered and absolutely liquid Cash Surplus which (unlike the capital and funds of an Insurance Company) is in no way under the control of the Member (i.e. the Insurer) but is held by Trustees in cash or Trustee Securities for the exclusive benefit of the Member's Policy holders.*

The minimum Deposit (which, of course, does not take into account the Member's Entrance Fee or the obligatory contribution to the Member's Premium Trust Fund*) is £5,000, but a Deposit of this amount would entitle a Member to transact Marine business only and that, of course, only up to a restricted amount. Unless, which is nowadays very unlikely, a Member were thus prepared to confine his operations solely to Marine business, he would be required to put up a supplementary Deposit in respect of the Non-Marine business in

---

* See page 99. This obligatory contribution is practically tantamount to an additional Deposit or permanent Reserve Fund.

which he desired to engage. To be able to transact what in the eyes of many at Lloyd's would be considered a quite modest volume of both Marine and Non-Marine Insurance a Member would have to put up Deposits of at least £8,000. Actually many Members have made individual Deposits which far exceed this figure, and at the present time, 1947, the total value of the Deposits thus held by the Corporation of Lloyd's is very considerably in excess of £24,000,000.

Machinery exists whereby the Committee is kept in close touch with the volume of business which is being transacted by any Member, and if at any time during any given year it looked as if the premium income of a Member were likely to exceed the limit to which he was entitled by virtue of his Deposit, he would either have to provide such further security as was demanded by the Committee or else cease doing any further business.

It is also to be observed that the whole of a Member's Deposit is held by the Corporation of Lloyd's as Trustee for the Member, his Executors, Administrators and Assigns, and that it is solely available as security for the Member's underwriting liabilities. Consequently, should the Member default no part of the Deposit will be released by the Committee except for the purpose of meeting that Member's *underwriting* liabilities, and only when these had been finally satisfied would any remaining portion of the Deposit become available for the defaulting Member's general creditors (as distinct from his Policyholders). Likewise, should a Member retire or die, the Committee would continue to hold his Deposit until finally satisfied that full provision had been made for all the underwriting liabilities of the retired or deceased Member. Even when it appeared evident that no further claims might be anticipated under policies which had been subscribed by the retired or deceased Member, the Committee will only release the Deposit against the receipt of a satisfactory Insurance Policy (usually arranged with other Lloyd's Underwriters) which in consideration of some agreed premium takes over all known and unknown liabilities under insurances which had been granted by the retired or deceased Member.

Premium Trust Fund.

Every Member has to sign a Trust Deed in a form approved by the British Government, whereby all premiums in respect of all insurances which he underwrites are placed in Trust Funds and until such time as all liabilities under these insurances have been paid or provided for, no part of these Trust Funds may be released by the Trustees except for the payment of underwriting expenses and claims which arise on these insurances.

It is important to note that under the terms of the Trust Deed the Funds, whether in the form of investments or cash, are exclusively and solely available for the underwriting liabilities of the Member, and that if the Member became insolvent no part of the Trust Fund could be attached by his General Creditors (as distinct from his Policyholders) unless and until all his liabilities to all his Policyholders had been fully satisfied.

It is also to be observed that as in the case of a Member's Deposit the Trustees hold his Premiums Trust Funds in trust for the payment of claims under policies of insurance subscribed by him and in the event of the death or retirement of the Member the trust does not cease until all his underwriting liabilities have been paid or provided for to the satisfaction of the Committee of Lloyd's.

From the foregoing it will be seen that none of the premiums paid or payable to a Member in respect of any Underwriting

Year* can be touched by him or by any parties other than the Trustees of his Premium Trust Funds until that Underwriting Year has been finally "closed." Thus, only actual and definitely ascertained profits can be released to a Member for his own use and then only with the consent and approval of the Trustees.

Another factor which should be mentioned is that before a Member is allowed to engage in any underwriting business he is required to make a payment of not less than £1000— which is quite independent of his Deposit—as an initial contribution towards his Premium Trust Funds. The original object of this requirement was to ensure that money belonging to the Member would be immediately available to the Underwriting Agent with which to meet any claims which might arise in the early days of the business while the Member's Premium Trust Funds are still in process of accumulating. Nowadays however this initial contribution is regarded and treated by the Committee as being in effect a permanent Reserve Fund—and if any of it is used for the payment of claims or expenses it must be built up again to its original amount before any profits are released to the Member.

Guarantees.

Under the provisions of the Assurance Companies Act, 1909, every Lloyd's Underwriter was required to furnish each year in respect of Non-Marine insurance business carried on by him security by way of deposit and/or guarantee up to 100 per cent of his premium income for the preceding year. This requirement was a domestic regulation of the Committee of Lloyd's prior to the 1909 Act and on the introduction of that Act it was embodied therein as a statutory obligation. With the amendment of the 1909 Act by the Assurance Companies Act, 1946, this requirement has been withdrawn

* See page 106.

as a statutory obligation, but it nevertheless continues as a domestic regulation of the Committee of Lloyd's, and thus Underwriters will revert to the position which existed prior to 1909.

That portion of the Member's deposit with the Corporation of Lloyd's which is specifically and primarily allocated to his Non-Marine business is regarded as providing a part of the security required under the foregoing regulation and the balance is furnished by means of a Guarantee Policy which, subject to very strict qualifications the Member secures from various other Lloyd's Underwriters. This is practically the only form of Financial Guarantee business which Lloyd's Underwriters (other than those few who have made special deposits in respect of Financial Guarantee Reinsurance business) are permitted to undertake, and they may only issue these Guarantee Policies within very strictly regulated limits.

Another very interesting and important feature about these Guarantee Policies is that contrary to all other Lloyd's Policies, the Lloyd's Underwriters who subscribe them make themselves *jointly and severally* liable up to the full amount of their respective subscriptions for the due carrying out of the guarantee which the Policy affords. Further, the amount tor which any one Member may thus guarantee another is limited to £200 and, equally important, no Member who carries on business through a given Underwriting Agent or Sub-Agent may guarantee another Member employing the same Underwriting Agent or Sub-Agent.

It will thus be seen that where a Member, in fulfilment of the regulations laid down by the Committee of Lloyds provides the Committee with a Guarantee Policy for, say, £10,000 in respect of his Non-Marine business for a given year, *this amount is divided over at least fifty other Members*

(i) *none* of whom employs the same Underwriting Agent or Sub-Agent as the Guaranteed Member, and

(ii) *each* of whom has complied with all the requirements of the British Government and the Committee of Lloyd's regarding individual Deposits and Premium Trust Funds, and

(iii) *each* of whom† is himself in turn guaranteed under like restrictions by other Members of Lloyd's.

Bearing in mind that at the beginning of each Underwriting Year* every Underwriting Member† has to provide a Guarantee Policy in respect of all Non-Marine insurances to be issued by him during that year, and that so long as he is doing business he will at any given moment always have three "unclosed" Underwriting Years (provided, of course, that he has been carrying on business for more than two years), it follows that three entirely separate Guarantee Policies in respect of that Underwriting Member will always be in force at any given moment—in other words, the total amount for which he is guaranteed is approximately *three* times the difference between (a) the amount of his annual Non-Marine premium income, and (b) the amount of his Non-Marine Deposit which is held by the Corporation of Lloyd's.

The Audit.

In the whole of the very comprehensive scheme of safeguards which exists for the protection of Holders of Lloyd's Policies, the most vital feature is, without question, the elaborate system of investigation of and control over the underwriting accounts and funds of every Lloyd's Underwriter.

It is certainly a matter for regret that when this system

---

* See page 106.
† If his annual Non-Marine premium income exceeds the amount of his Non-Marine Deposit.

H

of investigation and control of the underwriting accounts and funds of every Lloyd's Underwriter was first initiated in 1908 it was loosely and colloquially referred to at Lloyd's as "the Audit," and that this convenient but misleading appellation has ever since adhered to `it. In its ordinarily accepted sense the word "audit" implies little more than a thorough accounting process to check the correctness of balances on the basis of such information as is available or as is supplied to the Auditor—whereas an infinitely more exacting and drastic process is entailed in the system of investigation and control of Underwriting Accounts at Lloyd's which has come to be known as "the Audit."

It might briefly be described as a singular method designed for the purpose—which it has fulfilled in a very remarkable way—of ensuring that an individual who trades, or appears to be trading, in a manner which may involve him in financial difficulties is compelled to close down *before and not after* he has got into a position where he cannot meet his underwriting commitments.

No mere system of accountancy can achieve this remarkable result and it is maintained at Lloyd's that if other Organisations had in the past been subjected to measures of control comparable with "the Audit" as it exists at Lloyd's, various Insurance Companies whose eventual bankruptcy caused very serious losses to the public would have been compelled to stop business before they got into such low water that they could not meet their liabilities to their Policyholders.

The assertions and claims set out in the two last preceding paragraphs are very sweeping, and anyone making these would certainly be extremely foolish and doing the cause of Lloyd's more harm than good unless full substantiation of his statements was available. Since this Outline is primarily intended for the layman, who can hardly be expected to delve into or to appreciate all the intricacies of "the Audit "at Lloyd's, it is not within our province to attempt to set these out in detail but any Reader who desires further information and evidence on this question can easily obtain this from a Publication of the British Government.*

In the meantime it will suffice to say that as the result of "the Audit"

(*a*) each Member's Underwriting Accounts (which of course, are kept by his Underwriting Agent) are investigated annually by one of a panel of Certificated Accountants designated by the Committee of Lloyd's and composed of firms of the highest standing who specialise in dealing with the necessarily intricate accounts which are entailed in underwriting at Lloyd's.

(*b*) this Accountant, when making the investigation, conforms to certain very exacting rules which have been formulated by the Committee of Lloyd's with the special intention of enabling the Committee to obtain a correct picture of the state of the Member's underwriting business, these rules being constantly modified as experience shows that their effectiveness can be improved. If "the Audit" shows that the amount of a Member's underwriting Trust Funds falls short of a certain pre-determined ratio† of his premiums for any "unclosed" Underwriting Years—such ratio being fixed at a figure high enough to provide a satisfactory margin of safety—*then the Member must either provide out of his private resources such supplementary security as the Committee may require or else he must cease underwriting.*

---

* Minutes of Evidence taken on June 24th 1936 before the Departmental Committee on Compulsory Insurance appointed by the Board of Trade. Printed and published by H.M. Stationery Office.

† In actual practice separate accounts are kept for different classes of business and separate ratios are applied to these since manifestly the "lag" in the final settlement of claims varies in different classes.

(*Note.*—It will be observed that this is much the same as saying that if claims paid in respect of any "unclosed" Underwriting Years are above a predetermined and conservatively low datum line, this is regarded by the Committee as a warning, given in ample time, that the Member's financial position *might* become unsound if he continues his present style of operations.)

(*c*) this Accountant furnishes the Committee, which in turn furnishes the British Government (Board of Trade), with a Certificate in a form prescribed by the British Government that such Member's premiums are duly held in trust* and that his Underwriting Funds (apart from any of his other Assets) are sufficient to meet his underwriting liabilities.

When considering the foregoing the Reader should bear in mind that the actual accounting system obligatory on all Lloyd's Underwriters, while in some respects similar to the accounting systems employed by many Marine Insurance Companies is entirely different from that generally employed by almost all other Organisations transacting *Non-Marine* Insurance.

It requires that Claims and Return Premiums which become payable on policies *issued* in any given year (known at Lloyd's as an "Underwriting Year") shall be set against the Premiums received on *these* policies—which in effect means that each Underwriting Year has to stand on its own feet and that the Accounts for any given Underwriting Year are not closed until all liabilities incurred in that Underwriting Year have been finally determined.

* See page 99 (Premium Trust Fund).

The vast majority of other Insurance Organisations, however, work on the theory that it is possible to arrive at and to present a true picture of their financial position at the end of a Financial Year (as opposed to an Underwriting Year) by relying on a system in respect of the estimation of outstanding claims which depends very largely on what may be described as the personal element.

So far as it goes this latter theory is, of course, perfectly sound when applied by well-managed concerns, but even so, it is claimed for the Lloyd's system of accounting that quite independently of "the Audit" it has the great advantage of more quickly and more clearly bringing to light the true results of business actually *undertaken* in any given year.

Here it must be stressed that what may be termed the "Lloyd's system" of keeping accounts does not in itself constitute "the Audit"—but rather that the latter is built up on the very sound foundation which this system affords.

An accountant when auditing the accounts of any under-taking in the ordinary way, is essentially concerned with actual figures and with "approximations" with which he is provided—and so long as he does not disguise the fact that these latter are approximations it is not within his province to question how far the personal element may have come into play in arriving at these. Probably the most novel and striking feature of "the Audit" at Lloyd's is that it does not require the Accountant—or, far more important, the Member whose Underwriting Accounts are concerned or his Agent—to make any kind of approximations regarding the vital factor of Outstanding Claims, i.e., claims or possible claims which have been notified but which have not been settled.

It will be obvious, even to the veriest novice, let alone to an expert in Insurance matters, that the financial position of any Insurance Organisation at any given moment is very essentially affected by the extent or amount of the outstanding claims against it. Yet, at the same time, it will be equally obvious that its eventual liability in respect of these outstanding claims must, to a large degree, be a matter of guess work into which the personal element cannot but enter, since so long as a claim is unsettled or in dispute no one can accurately and definitely forecast its final outcome.

Now it can be accepted as a fact that in the case of any reputable and well-managed Insurance Organisation, those who are responsible for its management will adopt an honest and conservative attitude when making their guess as to the question of its possible liability in respect of outstanding claims. In such a case its published annual Profit and Loss Accounts and Balance Sheets or Financial Statements will afford to anyone who is versed in such matters a sufficiently accurate indication of its financial stability.

On the other hand, if those responsible for the management of an Insurance Organisation are unduly optimistic, even honestly so, or if they have reasons—as they patently will have if the concern is getting into low water—for wishing its financial position to appear in the most favourable possible light, then, notwithstanding all diligence on the part of an Auditor, and published estimate of its liability for outstanding claims may very easily prove to be unduly low. And who, outside the actual Management, can judge of this—until it is too late?

It is to guard against this possibility that under the Assurance Companies Act, 1946, every Insurance Company carrying on general insurance business (as defined in the Act) is required to show in its accounts for each year a surplus of assets over liabilities of £50,000 or 10 per cent of its premium income in respect of general insurance business for the last preceding year whichever be the greater.

Accumulated Reserves.

A notable feature of "the Audit" is that it does *not* take into account any Reserves which have been accumulated on behalf of a Member by his Underwriting Agent. It should here be explained that during the earlier years of a Member's underwriting activities it is usual for his Underwriting Agent to distribute only a certain proportion of any net profits which may have been earned for that Member—the balance being retained by the Underwriting Agent as an additional Reserve for that Member's future underwriting liabilities. This Reserve, although actually the property of the Member concerned (who draws the dividends thereon so long as all goes well) is normally held in the name of two Trustees who are empowered to release it only with the authority of the Underwriting Agent and only to such persons as the Underwriting Agent may designate—so that in the event of default on the part of a Member any additional Reserve so held by his Underwriting Agent may not become available for his General Creditors (as distinct from his Policyholders) until the Underwriting Agent is satisfied that the defaulting Member's underwriting liabilities have been fully liquidated.

It is known that for many Members there have thus been accumulated very substantial Reserves which, of course, constitute an extremely valuable, although undisclosed, source of strength.

Unlimited Personal Liability.

As has been mentioned before, every Lloyd's Underwriter—unlike the Shareholders or Members of an ordinary Joint Stock or Mutual Insurance Company—is personally liable up to the entire extent of his private fortune* for the due fulfilment of all commitments which he undertakes through issuing a Lloyd's Policy.

* See footnote on page 97.

Not only does this afford the utmost evidence of good faith but to all Lloyd's Policyholders it must obviously represent an immense safeguard, the cash and moral value of which one cannot even attempt to assess.

Central Guarantee Fund.

Whilst the corner-stone of the financial structure of Lloyd's is undoubtedly the Audit, which was introduced in 1908, the year 1926 was noteworthy for another most interesting and important development which came about after the discovery of a serious fraud perpetrated by a certain Member of Lloyd's whose criminal actions cost some of his fellow Members very dearly. Various steps of a far reaching nature were taken to prevent any future happening of this kind and in order further to safeguard the position it was decided to form the Central Guarantee Fund.

This Fund, which, it will be noted, was voluntarily brought into being at Lloyd's quite independently of any statutory requirements of the British Government is in addition to and in no way connected with the safeguards which all Members are required to provide individually and personally in the form of Premium Trust Funds and Deposits and Statutory Guarantees—all of which safeguards are, of course, in every case backed by the whole of the private fortunes of these individual Members.

The Central Guarantee Fund, which now amounts to over £1,750,000 in Securities or Cash, is under the sole control of the Committee of Lloyd's and it has been built up out of, and is ever being fed by, an annual levy on the premium income of all Lloyd's Underwriters.

Thus, in the remote event that any Member, despite the vigilance of "the Audit," should prove unable fully to meet his underwriting liabilities out of his Underwriting Funds and his private resources, any deficiency which arose could be made good by the Central Guarantee Fund.

Accordingly, although a Lloyd's Policy is so worded that the different Lloyd's Underwriters subscribing it are liable only "each for his own part and not one for another," it will be seen that in the financial structure of Lloyd's there is something very closely akin to corporate liability in that every Policy issued at Lloyd's has behind it the Central Guarantee Fund to which all Lloyd's Underwriters are contributors.

* * * *

Summing-up.

It has already been stressed that in considering the financial structure of Lloyd's the system of investigation and control known as "the Audit" must be regarded as the all-important feature. However, as the Reader will have realised, whilst this is in itself about as strong a safeguard to Lloyd's Policyholders as could be desired the actual security behind every Lloyd's Policy is far more than is brought about even by "the Audit."

Although the object of "the Audit" is, *inter alia*, to ensure that a Lloyd's Underwriter whose business is going badly will be compelled to stop underwriting whilst his Underwriting Funds are still sufficient to meet the whole of his underwriting liabilities, it is interesting to consider how the Holder of a Lloyd's policy would stand if it did indeed happen that one of the Underwriting Members subscribing this policy got into financial difficulties.

In such an eventuality liability for the payment of any sums due under the Policy from the defaulting Member would fall successively upon the following:—

(i) the Premium Trust Fund of the defaulting Member. (See page 99.)

(ii) any Reserves which the Underwriting Agent of the defaulting Member had accumulated on the latter's behalf. (See page 109.)

(iii) the personal fortune of the defaulting Member up to the last penny thereof. (See page 109.)

(iv) the Deposits made by the defaulting Member and held by the Corporation of Lloyd's in its own name. (See page 97.)

(v) the Central Guarantee Fund. (See page 110.)

(vi) the Lloyd's Underwriters who had subscribed such Statutory Guarantees as had been provided by and in respect of the defaulting Member. (See page 101.)

By reason of "the Audit" and the foregoing "Lines of Defence," it can justifiably be claimed that the security behind every Lloyd's Policy is unassailable and in keeping with the outstanding position which Lloyd's occupies in the Fields of Insurance.

INDEX